For Grades
# 5&6

# Write
## on Target

## Using Graphic Organizers
## to Improve Writing Skills

Written By:
Yolande F. Grizinski, Ed.D.
Leslie Holzhauser-Peters, MS, CCC-SP

Englefield & Arnold
Publishing

P.O. Box 341348
6344 Nicholas Drive
Columbus, OH 43234-1348

webpage: www.eapublishing.com
e-mail: eapub@eapublishing.com

1-877-PASSING
(614) 764-1211
fax: (614) 764-1311

**Published by:**
Englefield and Arnold, Inc.
P.O. Box 341348, 6344 Nicholas Drive
Columbus, OH 43234-1348
(614) 764-1211

Printed in the United States of America
05 04 03 02 01                    20 19 18 17 16 15 14 13 12 11 10 9 8 7 6 5 4 3 2 1

ISBN   1-884183-57-3

# About the Authors

**Yolande F. Grizinski** received a Bachelor's degree from Miami University, a Master's degree from Wright State University, and a Doctor of Education from the University of Cincinnati. She has worked in public education for twenty-six years as a curriculum consultant in the areas of language arts with a focus on writing assessment. She is currently the Assistant Superintendent of the Warren County Educational Service Center in Lebanon, Ohio.

**Leslie Holzhauser-Peters** holds a Bachelor's degree from the University of Cincinnati and Master's degree from Miami University. She has twenty-three years of experience working in public schools in Special Education and as a Speech-language pathologist, as a Supervisor, and currently as a Curriculum Consultant. Her areas of expertise are language, literacy, and intervention.

The authors met at the Warren County Educational Service Center and Lebanon, Ohio. There, they developed and implemented a host of language arts initiatives including a large-scale writing assessment. They have given numerous presentations on the five communication processes and Ohio's proficiencies.

In addition, the authors are the designers and trainers for the Collaborative Language and Literacy Intervention Demonstration Project that includes Dr. Catherine Snow as a consultant.

# Acknowledgements

The authors would like to acknowledge the works of Dr. Catherine Snow and Drs. Laura and Richard Kretschmer who have impacted their thinking about writing as a communication process.

**Englefield and Arnold Publishing acknowledges the following for their efforts in making this material available for students, parents, and teachers:**

Cindi Englefield Arnold, President/Publisher
Eloise Boehm-Sasala, Vice President/Managing Editor
Mercedes Baltzell, Production Editor
Bethany Hansgen, Project Editor
Scott D. Stuckey, Project Editor
Jennifer King, Illustrator/Cover Designer
Carissa Lipaj, Contributor


**Content Reviewers:**
Tammy Davis
Donna Holt
Carolyn O'Donnell
Judy Morgan


**Printer:**
McNaughton & Gunn, Inc.

# Table of Contents

# Table of Contents

# Table of Contents

# Foreword

We are fortunate to have worked with many wonderful educators and students in the years before writing this book. For the past ten years, we have examined over 40,000 student papers that were responses to prompts that provide students with on-demand writing tasks.

In our work, we have observed that many students have the ideas and motivation to complete the writing tasks asked of them but are unable to demonstrate appropriate writing skills. We have learned, through 12 years of large-scale writing assessment, that students often fall short in the organization of their thoughts and ideas. It was apparent in many cases that students did not have specific or organized structures "inside their heads" to plan their writing. As a result, their writing did not address the mode, was disorganized, shifted among purposes, and had weak endings. To improve students' organizational skills, we developed a graphic organizer for each of the 11 modes of writing. We tied each mode to one of five communication processes – narration, description, directions, explanation, and persuasion.

The model lesson format found in this book was demonstrated to classroom teachers with significant numbers of students at risk. These teachers used the model lesson format, modeling technique, and graphic organizers with their "at risk" students. After working for seven to eight months, these teachers found that their students' writing scores were the best in the building! Critical to this success was the ability of the classroom teacher to model the use of the graphic organizers over and over again, using clear examples for each mode of writing as a model.

Included in this book are descriptions of the five communication processes and 11 modes of writing, 22 model lessons, 22 prompts written with a purpose and an audience, 11 graphic organizers, student checklists, additional writing prompts, and a description of where students typically breakdown in the writing process.

The tools found in this book will serve students well as they work to improve their writing skills.

# Introduction

## What are Graphic Organizers?

Graphic organizers provide students with an organizational framework to help them plan their thinking and organize their thoughts. The use of graphic organizers increases the reader's and writer's comprehension of the text by providing a map to:

- find connections,
- organize large amounts of information,
- brainstorm ideas, and
- make decisions.

Each graphic organizer in this book shows the key parts of the communication process and the relationship of these parts to the whole.

The greatest challenge some students face is their ability to organize their writing into an orderly framework that is understood by the reader. In both reading and writing, students are asked to interpret and comprehend meaning. The graphic organizer is a tool that can assist students during the reading and writing process. While reading with the graphic organizer, students can increase their comprehension by using the graphic organizer to trace the organization of the reading selection. While writing with the graphic organizer, students can place their own ideas and thoughts into a structure that fits the purpose of the prompt.

## Using Graphic Organizers to Succeed

This book provides fifth and sixth grade classroom teachers with a lesson plan framework for teaching writing skills to promote student success.

Five specific communication processes (narration, description, directions, explanation, and persuasion) have been selected and paired with specific graphic organizers for instructional use.

The five communication processes can be further broken down into eleven writing modes. (A description of each mode can be found in Preface One.) In order for students to be successful writers, they must be skillful in responding to eleven different types (modes) of writing.

## Successful Results with Graphic Organizers

We saw significant improvement when graphic organizers were used in both regular classroom instruction and large-scale, on-demand writing assessments. Students are able to understand information, organize their thoughts, and stay focused on their writing.

When the appropriate graphic organizer is used, teachers are able to trace a student's thinking during the planning stage of writing. After using the graphic organizer, we see an improved organizational structure in students' work with a clear beginning, middle, and end. Students are able to write to the purpose of the mode even when the students' final products are not fully developed. Teachers can see where students breakdown in the writing process and plan intervention.

## Targeted Areas to Improve

Through our experiences in scoring and reflecting on students' writing samples, we recognize there is a significant need to improve student writing content, organization, and clarity in addressing a prompt. We observed that student papers often contained problems including:

- no clear ending or sense of closure;
- shifts among the communication processes (for example, students moved between personal narrative and directions);
- ideas that were presented randomly with no sequence or organization;
- no clear sense of purpose for the mode; and/or
- did not address the audience (reader).

## Holistic Scores Improve

We could see the development of wonderful ideas on topics by students when graphic organizers were presented. We found that their holistic scores improved with significant gains in content and organization when:

1. The same lesson plan framework was used for any writing task.
2. The graphic organizer was tailored to match the purpose of the writing prompt.
3. The same set of graphic organizers was used over and over again so that students developed consistency when writing to the basic communication processes.

# Ways to Use *Write on Target* in Your Writing Program

## Primary Purpose

The primary purpose of this book is to enable students to understand the unique features of each of the five communication processes (narration, description, directions, explanation, and persuasion) and to practice eleven modes of writing.

*Write on Target* has graphic organizers that match eleven modes of writing. Each graphic organizer was developed to incorporate those components of the mode that make it unique and different from the others. The goal in having students use graphic organizers is to provide them with an organizational framework that allows them to learn and integrate the characteristics and components of each mode. The goal is to use the same graphic organizer any time the student is to write or speak using that particular mode. If students are asked to use a different graphic organizer each time they write or speak, the purpose is defeated.

Students may not understand how to use graphic organizers initially. They often use the graphic organizers to write out their entire paper rather than as a planning guide.

## In addition, Write on Target can also be used:

1. as a major component of a **year-long writing program**. Students would complete two prompts for each of the eleven modes in either grade five or grade six.

2. as a **pre- or post-assessment** for each of the eleven modes of writing for a particular grade level.

3. as an **assessment portfolio** that would move with each student from grade five to grade six (eleven prompts covering the eleven modes in grade five; eleven prompts covering the eleven modes in grade six).

4. as a **bank of prompts** that supports regular classroom instruction.

5. as support for concentrated **standardized test preparation** programs.

6. as a **summer school writing program** or as part of an **intervention program**.

7. as **on-demand writing tasks** for **individualized practice**.

## Guidelines for Using the Graphic Organizer

1. Model the use of the graphic organizer by thinking through the planning of a written piece.

2. Model the completion of the graphic organizer by inserting a word, phrase, picture, or abbreviation in each box. This modeling process needs to occur over and over again. Explain to students the purpose of the graphic organizer. Students need to know that their time and energy should be reserved for writing their own piece.

3. Model how to transfer thoughts organized on the graphic organizer into a written piece.

4. Share the rubrics used for scoring with the students. Student models of the various rubric levels (4, 3, 2, 1, 0) should be shared regularly with students.

# Ways to Use *Write on Target* in Your Reading Program

In addition to the writing process, the graphic organizer can be used to assist comprehension during the reading process. Given a fiction or nonfiction text to read silently, students will demonstrate an understanding of text and elements of fiction or nonfiction by responding to items in which they:

## I. Comprehend Fiction and Nonfiction Selections

- to assess what a student knows about a topic (prior knowledge)

- to organize ideas in reading materials

- to gain an understanding of the structure of a specific communication process (purpose)

- to guide and focus students' thinking during class discussion of student writing or reading materials

## A. Examine aspects of text in fiction and nonfiction.

This objective focuses on analyzing elements in a fiction text such as:
- Characters
- Setting
- Plot
- Problem (or conflict)
- Solution (or resolution)
- Point of View
- Theme

This objective focuses on analyzing elements in a nonfiction text such as:
- Comparison and Contrast
- Cause and Effect
- Fact or Opinion

## B. Give a brief summary of the text.

Using interpretations and reactions to a text selection, a student should be able to construct, in his/her own words, a brief summary that highlights important parts of the selection.

## C. Make an inference from the text.

Using ideas and clues from the text, students should be able to draw conclusions that are not implicitly stated in the text.

## II. Interpret Fiction and Nonfiction Selections

- to facilitate text comprehension by making new connections

- to see how things are related

- to organize personal reactions, thoughts, and feelings

- to create original products to fit a specific communication process (purpose)

## A. Respond to the text.

Students describe their own personal experiences or feelings by responding through discussion or writing.

## B. Compare and contrast aspects of the text.

- In fiction, students notice aspects of the text, such as setting or conflict, that are similar or different. These comparisons help students make important discoveries or realizations about the text.

- In nonfiction, students notice aspects of the text, aside from ones specifically discussed by the author, that are similar or different.

## C. Discuss the appropriateness of the text for a specific audience or purpose.

Students recognize different types of audiences and purposes and address the appropriateness of each.

## D. Explain how an author uses the text to support his/her purpose for writing.

Students determine the author's purpose for writing and address how he/she uses the text to support that purpose.

# Modes Of Writing

## What Writing Skills Should Fifth and Sixth Graders Have?

By the time students reach fifth and sixth grade, they are expected to write for a variety of purposes and to a variety of audiences. These eleven modes of writing prepare students to write for school success and prepare them for life skills.

### Eleven Modes of Writing:

1. **Fictional narrative** – a piece of writing that is a made-up story that could appear to be true to the reader. It contains named characters, a title, events that detail what happens, and establishes an inferred or explicit problem. A fictional narrative is comprised of a beginning, a middle, and an end.

2. **Personal experience narrative** – a piece of nonfiction writing that is a believable story based on the student's own life experience. Within the narrative, details can be found that relate who was there, when it happened, and/or where it occurred. Like a fictional narrative, a personal experience narrative has a title, and is made up of a beginning, a middle, and an end.

3. **Journal** – a piece of writing recounting the activities of a day, a month, or a year. Included within the journal should be the date, a description of the sights, sounds, people, and events around the writer, and a description of the writer's feelings. Often, the audience for a journal is oneself. A journal may be written in letter or paragraph form.

4. **Letter** – a piece of writing, organized in the correct style of a letter (including a greeting, a body, and a closing), that addresses a specific audience with the intention of establishing a written connection or communication with them.

5. **Directions** – a piece of writing explaining how to do something (*e.g.*, how to go somewhere, or how to make something). Using step-by-step order, the directions should clearly describe the materials that are necessary to complete the task. It may be written in paragraph form or line-by-line, but must include a starting point and an ending point.

## Eleven Modes of Writing (continued):

6. **Invitation** – a piece of writing, possibly in the form of a letter, that includes the following information: the purpose of the invitation, who is writing the invitation, who is being invited, where they are being invited to, when they are being invited, and any other important information.

7. **Informational** – a piece of nonfiction writing based upon researched facts. Its purpose is to inform the audience about a topic (the topic can cover a wide variety of subjects) the author has learned about. This mode of writing is presented in an organized format consisting of a beginning, a middle, and an end, and is written in the student's own words.

8. **Summary** – a piece of writing that identifies what the text selection is about and states the main ideas of the text selection. It does not include information that is not important and has fewer details than a retelling.

9. **Thank-You Note** – a piece of writing in the form of a letter, including a greeting, a body and a closing, that explains what the writer is thankful for and why.

10. **Letter to the Editor** – a piece of writing in the form of a letter, including greeting, body and closing, that expresses the writer's opinion and why it is important. The writer's opinion should be based on facts, examples and/or reasons. The writer should also include what he/she would like to see happen.

11. **Persuasive** – a piece of writing that states a position on an issue and attempts to convince the audience to agree with the writer. This is accomplished by providing supporting evidence or reasons for the position taken based on facts. An important part of a persuasive piece is anticipating the other side's point of view.

# Using Graphic Organizers

## The Model Lesson

There are four major components key to any good lesson that incorporates graphic organizers. These four components include:

1. **Prior Knowledge** – to determine the student's prior knowledge about the topic, purpose, or task of the lesson.

2. **Model** – to model the use of the graphic organizer through class discussion with the thinking process modeled aloud as the organizer is completed.

3. **Guided Practice** – to provide guided practice by presenting a task for students to complete that matches the purpose of the graphic organizer you want to teach.

4. **Independent Practice** – to provide independent practice so students are provided with on-demand writing tasks that are organized according to the purpose.

## Defining Each Component of the Model Lesson

### I.  Determining Prior Knowledge of Students

Students must make personal connections with the purpose of the material being presented. Establishing a student's familiarity with the material is important for interpreting and comprehending meaning and ultimately retaining information. The following questions can be used with any lesson to tap into prior knowledge of the whole class or for an individual student:

1. What do you know about _____? (The student response provides the teacher with an assessment of what he or she knows prior to the lesson.)

2. Where do you see this in your life? (The student response helps to establish the importance of the task for now and for the future.)

Both of these questions show how students are connected with the material. This process is important for the retention of information. Students need to make connections themselves.

> ## Sample Questions to Tap Prior Knowledge
>
> - Does anyone know what a narrative is?
> - What do we know about narratives?
> - What are some parts of a narrative?
> - What is the narrative's purpose? or audience?
> - Who reads or writes narratives?
> - Where do you see narratives every day?
> - What does personal mean?
> - What is a personal narrative?

## II. Modeling

Modeling or demonstrating the thinking process for the use of the selected graphic organizer is an important component of any lesson. Modeling must be done frequently because it is the part of the lesson by which students construct meaning.

### There are two types of modeling

1. Demonstrating the thinking process used in completing a graphic organizer.
2. Providing samples of both acceptable and unacceptable writing keyed to the scoring rubric. (The scoring rubric can be found on page 13.)

Both types of modeling must be done frequently. Time is well spent during the modeling phase of the lesson. Modeling clarifies the task and enables the student to internalize the standard.

The model needs to match the purpose of the writing task the students will complete. Written models can be obtained from a variety of sources (see chart on the next page). Once you become aware of the writing modes, you and your students will be able to select written models from a variety of sources:

- newspapers
- trade books
- textbooks
- student generated models*

\* Over time, develop a bank of students' responses that are good examples of the different types of writing modes; include different levels of the scoring rubric.

# The Five Communication Processes
# Matched with Eleven Writing Modes

| Communication Process | Eleven Writing Modes | Sources of Modes |
|---|---|---|
| Narrative | Fictional Narratives | magazines, trade books, literature-based reading series |
| | Personal Experience Narratives | newspapers, diaries, journals |
| Description* | Journals | diaries, journals, science reports, advertisements |
| | Letters | personal correspondence, published documents |
| Directions | Directions | recipes, stage directions, maps |
| | Invitations | weddings, birthdays, parties, formal and informal formats |
| Explanation | Informational Reports | business reports, science and social studies text-books, newspapers, and magazines |
| | Summaries | movie reviews, book jackets, encyclopedia |
| | Thank-You Notes | personal correspondence |
| Persuasion | Letters to the Editor | newspapers, magazines, advertisements, commercials |
| | Persuasive | newspapers, magazines, advertisements, commercials |

\* Note: The ability to describe is an important skills embedded in many of the communication processes and writing modes.

## III. Guided Practice

During guided practice, the teacher should provide various levels of support to students as needed.

Provide a task for students to complete that matches what it is you want to teach in the most authentic way possible. For example, have students write a persuasive letter to the editor of the newspaper regarding an issue facing the school or community, or ask students to write a set of directions to be followed.

After considerable guided practice, provide students with many opportunities to engage in independent practice with "on-demand" writing prompts. Sample prompts are included at the end of each chapter of this book.

## IV. Independent Practice

Independent practice is an "on-demand" task that provides students with a test-like writing experience. During independent practice, students should be given a graphic organizer, a writing prompt with a specific purpose, a writing model (optional), lined paper, and a writing checklist. It is important that teachers provide enough time for students to complete the writing task.

During independent practice, no teacher or peer assistance should be provided to students. No reference materials can be used. Independent practice is different from lessons that take students through all stages of the writing process. These student papers are considered rough drafts and scored accordingly with the scoring rubric. It is critical that students be provided with this type of task on many occasions throughout the school year.

The "on-demand" writing task is designed so that students can choose to use either print or cursive formats. The students should choose the format that is most comfortable to them. Every attempt should be made to determine the meaning and content of each student's paper. Legibility issues should be minimized whenever possible.

After the students have completed this type of independent practice, it is the role of the teacher to return to the model lesson and cycle through the lesson again before the next independent practice is presented to the class.

# Rubric for Holistic Scoring of Student Writing

The scoring of papers is designed to focus on the most important features. The writer's ability to transmit meaning to the reader by writing to the purpose with a strong organization is considered most important and given most value.

**Weighting of Writing Features**

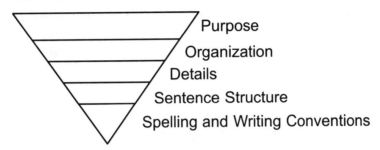

Purpose
Organization
Details
Sentence Structure
Spelling and Writing Conventions

A **4-point** response clearly addresses the topic and purpose, and has ample supporting detail. It is logically organized and includes a beginning, a middle, and an end. The student utilizes language effectively by using a variety of words and sentence patterns. For the most part, punctuation, capitalization, and spelling are correct, and any error does not hinder the flow or meaning of the response. An attempt at creating a personal style as well as a realization of an audience are noticeable.

A **3-point** response generally addresses the topic and purpose with some supporting detail. The response is organized logically with a beginning, a middle, and an end. There are attempts to use a variety of words and sentence patterns. Some errors in sentence structure, spelling, punctuation, and/or capitalization occur, but they do not hinder the flow or meaning of the response.

A **2-point** response attempts to address the topic and purpose but may stray from the main point. Few details are used to support the response, and extraneous information may be included. Ideas are organized in an undeveloped form that lacks a complete beginning, middle, and/or ending (often does not include a sense of closure). Most sentences are capitalized and punctuated correctly with some errors. Some commonly used words are misspelled which causes interference with the message of the response.

A **1-point** response minimally addresses the topic or purpose. It shows little or no organizational pattern and presents limited detail. It uses sentence patterns or language that greatly interfere with the meaning. There are more than a few instances of capitalization and punctuation being used incorrectly. Incorrect spelling obscures the meaning of the response.

An **unscorable** response is a paper that does not fit into any of the above categories. These individual cases may include papers that are: illegible, off topic, written in a  foreign language, blank.

# Model Lesson: Putting It All Together, Step-by-Step

Writing activities for each writing mode are arranged step-by-step in the Parent/Teacher Edition and Student Workbook. The following steps are derived from the four components of the Model Lesson. Each time you teach a lesson, you may want to refer to these steps. This model lesson guide is directly matched to the writing activities in the chapters that follow.

## Prior Knowledge

Before you begin, ask students, "What do you know about (*insert one of the eleven writing modes, e.g., fictional narrative*)? Where have you seen this in your life?"

## Model

**Step 1:**
- Introduce a model text selection that is typical of the writing mode you are describing.
- Read the model and highlight its features.
- Show the graphic organizer that corresponds to the writing mode. (Full size graphic organizers can be found throughout the Student Workbook.)
- Use the model text selection to complete the graphic organizer.
- Explain how the graphic organizer should be used by completing the graphic organizer on an overhead, or by providing each student with a personal copy.
- As a class, demonstrate the completion of the graphic organizer using a think-aloud technique.

**Step 2:** Discuss the characteristics of the communication process you are introducing.

# Model Lesson: Putting It All Together, Step-by-Step

## Guided Practice

**Step 3:** Introduce the prompt students will be addressing as well as the appropriate graphic organizer. Students should think about how they will address the prompt.

**Step 4:** Students will complete the graphic organizer based on the prompt. The graphic organizer will help students arrange their thoughts.

**Step 5:** Each student will complete the writing activity based on the prompt and the information he or she has organized with the graphic organizer.

**Step 6:** The checklist provided in this section shows what a student's best paper must have. Students should use this checklist as a guideline for their responses.

## Independent Practice

Once students have completed the six steps, they are ready for independent practice. Provide students with on-demand writing tasks. Refer to the additional prompts, specific to each mode, found at the end of each chapter of this book. (For more information on independent practice, refer to Section IV on page 12.)

The final step is scoring student papers. Score the papers based on the scoring rubric. Students should become familiar with the standards of the four-point rubric.

# Design Your Own Writing Prompts

## Guidelines to Consider

1. **A clear purpose must be specified.** Choose the writing mode you want to test and tell the students what they are expected to do. Use words such as "describe," "persuade," or "summarize" in the directions. Keep the prompt as simple as possible. Prompts should be comprised of words your students can easily read and understand. The writing test should not become a reading test.

2. **The audience should be indicated.** The audience should be a person or a group the students would feel comfortable addressing. Often, for the purposes of the writing assessment, teacher scorers are the audience.

3. **Students should have a solid prior knowledge base about the topic before they begin writing.** The subject matter of the writing prompt should be within the realm of each student's experience and should not involve emotionally-charged issues that would distract from the writing task. For example, not all students have visited Canada. Asking students to describe the landscape of Canada would be unfair to those students who have not experienced the Canadian landscape firsthand. An alternative might be to ask students to describe their idea of a beautiful landscape.

4. **The evaluation criteria and prompt checklist should be reviewed with students before administering of the on-demand writing task.** The scoring rubric should not be a mystery to students. Students need to develop a clear understanding of the standard and scoring procedures. We have found that students become excellent scorers when trained to use the rubric.

# Chapter 1

# The Narrative Communication Process
## (Fictional Narrative and Personal Experience Narrative)

## The Key Parts of this Chapter Include:

**1** Discussing the purpose and features of a fictional narrative and a personal experience narrative.

**2** Showing how the narrative communication process links the eleven writing modes.

**3** Offering teaching tips on where students breakdown in the narrative process.

**4** Providing ideas for the development of additional writing prompts for the fictional narrative and the personal experience narrative.

---

The following teaching tools are provided for a **fictional narrative** and a **personal experience narrative**: graphic organizers, models, two writing prompts, and student checklists.

---

## What is the Narrative Communication Process?

The purpose of the narrative communication process is to tell a story. A fictional narrative is a made-up story. The personal experience narrative is an account of an event that could have happened to the writer in real life.

### Feature of a Fictional Narrative

- A fictional narrative is a made-up story that has a central problem.

Narrative Communication information for students can be found on page 1 of the *Write on Target* Student Workbook.

### Features of the Personal Experience Narrative

- A personal experience narrative is typically told in the first person ("I").
- A personal experience narrative focuses on an event that could have happened to the writer in real life.

## Correlation of Narrative Communication to the Writing Modes

**Fictional narrative** – a piece of writing that is a made-up story that could appear to be true to the reader. It contains named characters, a title, events that detail what happens, and establishes an inferred or explicit problem.  A fictional narrative is comprised of a beginning, middle, and end.

**Personal experience narrative** – a piece of nonfiction writing that is a believable story based on the student's own life experience. Within the narrative, details can be found that relate who was there, when it happened, and/or where it occurred. Like a fictional narrative, a personal experience narrative has a title, and is made up of a beginning, middle, and end.

## Teaching Tips:
## Where Students Breakdown in the Narrative Communication Process

- Students write the story as they would verbally tell it, so it is not organized in a sequential fashion.

- Students make assumptions that the reader has had the same experience. Students leave out essential information for the reader.

- Students include too much or too little information that takes away from the storyline.

- Students do not stay with the purpose.

- Students confuse personal experience narrative with fictional narrative. The personal experience narrative should include an event that could or did happen.

- Students do not always have a clear beginning, middle, or end.

# Writing Activity 1: Fictional Narrative
## (A Made-Up Story)

*Step*

# 1

Follow along as the fictional narrative "Lucky" is read aloud.

### Lucky

Lucky was not just any dog; Lucky was Jeremy's best friend. "Before you know it, that dog will be sitting down to dinner with the entire family," said Jeremy's mother as she tried to hide her smile. "How many times do I have to tell you? Lucky is just a dog." Since the stray golden retriever found his way to Jeremy's front porch four years ago, Lucky and the boy were inseparable.

Early one Monday morning, Jeremy sleepily sifted out the few bits of cereal left floating in his bowl full of milk. Lucky gently placed one paw in his owner's lap. "All right, boy, you can finish the rest." The golden retriever lapped up the sweet milk and looked at Jeremy with his large, brown eyes that always seemed to say, 'Thank you, friend.'

Before rushing off to school, Jeremy hugged Lucky good-bye on his way out the door. He locked the gate behind him as he ran toward the rumbling, yellow school bus that stood waiting for him.

Upon returning home that afternoon, Jeremy realized something was terribly wrong. The gate was open, and Lucky was gone! Jeremy dropped his books and began to run down the street shouting for Lucky. He called Lucky's name until his throat was sore. He stopped at every house in the neighborhood, but no one had seen Lucky. Jeremy somberly returned home.

At dinner, Jeremy pushed the mashed potatoes around on his blue plate; he could hardly look out the window at the empty yard. "Go on, see if you can find Lucky before dark," Jeremy's mother said reluctantly as she took his plate from the table.

Remembering the times he and Lucky played ball and swam in the lake, Jeremy quickly pedaled toward the water. Lucky had always enjoyed playing there. When Jeremy reached the lake, he called out Lucky's name, desperate to find his friend. From behind a cluster of cattails came the sound of a deep bark. When the dog appeared, he was covered with mud that he eagerly shared with a smiling Jeremy. "Let's go home, boy." Lucky ran alongside Jeremy's bike as they traveled home. Jeremy realized how "lucky" he was to find his Lucky.

*Step* **2**

There are several things to keep in mind as you plan and write your own fictional narrative (A Made-Up Story). Remember, a good fictional narrative (A Made-Up Story) has the following parts:

- a title that fits the story
- a character or characters you can picture in your mind
- a problem that a character needs to solve
- a beginning, middle, and end (think about what happens first, next, then, and finally)

*Step* **3**

Use the following prompt to complete the prewriting and writing activities:

**Write a fictional narrative. Your narrative begins when your main character is walking in the woods and hears a noise coming from the treetops. Tell what happens in the story.**

*Step* **4**

Complete the graphic organizer for a fictional narrative as your prewriting activity. Use your graphic organizer to help you think through your fictional narrative.

*A full size graphic organizer can be found on page 4 of the Student Workbook.*

**FICTIONAL NARRATIVE**

A Made-Up Story

Title: _____

| Who: |
| Where: |
| When: |

| What Is The Problem? |

| What Happened? | First: |

| What Happened? | Next: |

| What Happened? | Then: |

| Finally: |

**Step 5**

Use the information from your graphic organizer to complete your fictional narrative. *(Students will have two pages to complete their writing activities.)*

### Writing Activity 1

_____

_____

_____

_____

_____

**Step 6**

The checklist shows what your best paper must have. Use the checklist below to review your work.

### Checklist for Writing Activity 1

☐ My story has a title.

☐ My characters have names.

☐ My story begins when the main character hears a noise in the woods.

☐ My story gives details about what happened after my main character heard the noise.

☐ My fictional narrative is well organized and complete.

☐ I try to spell words correctly.

☐ I use words that make my meaning clear. I do not use the same words over and over.

☐ I use correct punctuation and capitalization.

☐ I have written my story so the reader can read my print or cursive writing.

# Writing Activity 2: Fictional Narrative
## (A Made-Up Story)

*Step*
*1*

Follow along as the fictional narrative "Lions and Tigers and Cheetahs" is read aloud.

### Lions and Tigers and Cheetahs

Sitting at her desk, Amanda opened her science book to a picture of her favorite animal, the cheetah. Deep in thought, she traced her finger around the edge of the spotted cat's photograph. Amanda was startled as her teacher called the class to line up for the field trip to the zoo. With sack lunches, cool drinks, and comfortable shoes, the class started on their journey. Walking among her classmates, Amanda heard her spending money for the zoo gift shop jingling in her pocket.

The zoo was divided into continents: Australia, Asia, North America, Africa, and South America. Amanda was anxious to see everything, but she really wanted to see the fascinating cheetah. Amanda followed along several pathways as she passed African elephants, wildebeests, giraffes, and the rare black rhinoceros.

The pathway eventually led Amanda to a sign with the small, black letters that read "CHEETAH." As she approached the exhibit area, she saw a spotted animal sitting in the tall grass. She watched as the cheetah stood and stretched its long, thin legs. It looked just like its photograph with small, rounded ears and a narrow, white chest. Its coat was yellowish-gray with solid, black spots. Amanda noticed a dark streak on the animal's face extending from the corner of each eye to its upper lip.

Suddenly, the cheetah began to run fast, then faster. Its legs seemed to dig into the earth as it became a blur before her eyes. The magnificent cheetah ran across the land with incredible speed. The animal suddenly stopped at the crest of the hill and turned toward Amanda. She and the animal locked eyes for a brief moment before the cheetah disappeared over the small mound of earth. She gasped and silently said goodbye.

The class ended their field trip with a visit to the gift shop. It was filled with rubber snakes, koala stuffed animals, board games, and books on every possible animal topic. Amanda looked around and noticed a jar wrapped with a cheetah's picture. A small sign pleaded, "Help the endangered cheetah." Amanda fingered the money from her pocket. She carefully put the entire amount into the jar and whispered, "What a beautiful animal. It's so sad the cheetahs are almost extinct."

*Step* **2**
There are several things to keep in mind as you plan and write your own fictional narrative (A Made-Up Story). Remember, a good fictional narrative (A Made-Up Story) has the following parts:

- a title that fits the story
- a character or characters you can picture in your mind
- a problem that a character needs to solve
- a beginning, middle, and end (think about what happens first, next, then, and finally)

*Step* **3**
Use the following prompt to complete the prewriting and writing activities:

**You will write a fictional narrative. Your characters will have the opportunity to meet a famous musical entertainer, television personality, book character, author, or historical figure. Tell a story about what happens to your characters when they meet this famous person.**

*Step* **4**
Complete the graphic organizer for a fictional narrative as your prewriting activity. Use your graphic organizer to help you think through your fictional narrative.

*A full size graphic organizer can be found on page 10 of the Student Workbook.*

**FICTIONAL NARRATIVE**

A Made-Up Story

Title: _____

Who:
Where:
When:

What Is The Problem?

What Happened? | First:

What Happened? | Next:

What Happened? | Then:

Finally:

*Step*
**5**

Use the information from your graphic organizer to complete your fictional narrative. *(Students will have two pages to complete their writing activities.)*

## Writing Activity 2

_____

_____

_____

_____

_____

*Step*
**6**

The checklist shows what your best paper must have. Use the checklist below to review your work.

## Checklist for Writing Activity 2

- ☐ My story has a title.
- ☐ My characters have names.
- ☐ My story gives the name of the famous person the characters meet.
- ☐ My story tells what happens when my characters meet the famous person.
- ☐ My fictional narrative is well organized and complete.
- ☐ I try to spell words correctly.
- ☐ I use words that make my meaning clear. I do not use the same words over and over.
- ☐ I use correct punctuation and capitalization.
- ☐ I have written my story so that my reader can read my print or cursive writing.

# Writing Activity 3: Personal Experience Narrative (A Story About Me)

*Step*
*1*
Follow along as the personal experience narrative "The Big Change" is read aloud.

## The Big Change

We pulled up to the gigantic brick building, and I slowly opened the van door, pushing myself out onto the sidewalk. "Bye," I said dejectedly.

"Have a great day," my mom replied cheerfully when I slammed the heavy passenger side door shut. I watched our van slowly creep out of the parking lot. I turned around to see a long row of steps leading up to two enormous wooden doors. Unfamiliar students rushed by me, laughing and talking, making their way into the building. I urged my legs forward and up the numerous steps. I shakily reached to pull the handle of the left door, but it flung open without my touching it. A stream of new faces brushed past me and down the stairs. "New girl," I heard someone say as I quickly made my way through the door on the right.

I stepped through to see people weaving through the long hallway. Lockers surrounded me as I hurried through the noise and sea of faces. My eye caught a short blonde girl smiling at me from down the corridor. Making my way toward her, I noticed she was standing under a sign that said "Guidance Office" in bold, white letters.

"I'm Ashley," she said, warmly giving me a smile. "Are you Karen? I have heard so much about you," she declared, not giving me a chance to answer. "I volunteered to show you around. I was new at this school last year and felt really nervous about my first day. I am here to make your first day a little easier."

"Thanks," I stammered. "I have no idea where to go." My heart rate slowed. I felt better and less nervous than when I first arrived. Ashley showed me around the entire day. She introduced me to all my new teachers and classmates. The other students were very friendly, and I felt at ease in my new school. Ashley was quick to let me know about an important school tradition, "Always use the right door. Whether you're entering or exiting, you'll always be in the 'right' if you use the right door." We both laughed when I told her I learned that lesson the hard way. Maybe this new school won't be so bad after all, I thought to myself.

*Step*
2

Now you will do some organizing and planning for your own personal experience narrative (A Story About Me). Write about something that could or did happen to you in your life. The prewriting graphic organizer will help you get ideas for your story. Remember that a personal experience narrative (A Story About Me) has the following parts:

- a title that fits the story
- people you know, or events, special times, and memories that did or could have happened to you in real life
- a beginning, middle, and end (think about what happens first, next, then, and finally)

*Step*
3

Use the following prompt to complete the prewriting and writing activities:

> **You arrived home from school and opened the door. You were not prepared for the big surprise that was about to happen to you. Tell a story to a friend about this surprising time.**

*Step*
4

Complete the graphic organizer for a personal experience narrative as your prewriting activity. Use your graphic organizer to help you think through your personal experience narrative.

*A full size graphic organizer can be found on page 16 of the Student Workbook.*

**PERSONAL EXPERIENCE NARRATIVE**

A Story About Me

Title: _____

| Who was there? |
| Where did it happen? |
| When did it happen? |

| What Took Place? | First: |
| What Took Place? | Next: |
| What Took Place? | Then: |

| Finally: |

**Step 5**

Use the information from your graphic organizer to complete your personal experience narrative. *(Students will have two pages to complete their writing activities.)*

### Writing Activity 3

_____

_____

_____

_____

_____

**Step 6**

The checklist shows what your best paper must have. Use the checklist below to review your work.

### Checklist for Writing Activity 3

- ☐ My story has a title.
- ☐ My story is about a time when I was surprised.
- ☐ My story begins when I open the door.
- ☐ My story gives details about why I was surprised.
- ☐ My story has a beginning, middle, and end.
- ☐ My personal experience narrative is well organized and complete.
- ☐ I try to spell words correctly.
- ☐ I use words that make my meaning clear. I do not use the same words over and over.
- ☐ I use correct punctuation and capitalization.
- ☐ I have written my story so that my reader can read my print or cursive writing.

# Writing Activity 4: Personal Experience Narrative
# (A Story About Me)

*Step*

# 1

Follow along as the personal experience narrative "Yosemite" is read aloud.

## Yosemite

As Terrance's dad drove us closer to Yosemite National Park, I was so excited. I had never been out West before. As the car slid past the park's entrance, I pressed my face against the window to take in the scenery. This was not like the parks back in Cleveland. Even the metroparks, which I always thought were pretty big, were small compared to Yosemite. "Over 700,000 acres in size," Terrance's mom read from a sign.

Terrance's dad drove deep into the park, then stopped at a place called Crane's Flat. Terrance and I leapt from our seats; we were so glad to stand and stretch after that long car ride. It felt like we had been in the car for a month straight! I was elated when Terrance's parents told us we were walking to Tuolumne Grove. I had no idea what Tuolumne Grove was, but I was happy we didn't have to be in the car to get there.

With our feet in comfortable shoes and packs on our backs, we headed for the grove. Terrance and I kept our eyes on the ground. We were looking for insects. Terrance hoped to find some intriguing creatures he had never seen before for his collection. We were so busy bug hunting, we did not notice we were falling behind his parents.

Walking deeper into the grove, the sun seemed to be disappearing, so I looked up. I nudged Terrance, who was busy looking at a beetle. Our mouths dropped. We were surrounded by a forest of the biggest trees I had ever seen, and the Smiths were nowhere to be found. I started to panic. Yosemite was so big. If we're lost, no one will ever find us, I thought. I should have stayed closer to Terrance's parents. What would my parents say if the Smiths came home without me?

"Hey guys, over here," I heard Mrs. Smith call. We both looked around but didn't see her anywhere. She called again, but I still couldn't spot her. When I heard Mr. Smith laughing, I turned in his direction. Terrance's parents were walking around a giant sequoia. The tree had to be 75 feet around! I felt pretty stupid for being so worried, but I was relieved to see them. Terrance's mom took my picture next to the giant trees. I couldn't wait to show the picture to my family, but I knew they'd laugh when I told them about losing Terrance's parents behind a tree.

Tall Tree Forest

*Step*
**2**
Now you will do some organizing and planning for your own personal experience narrative (A Story About Me). Write about something that could or did happen to you in your life. The prewriting graphic organizer will help you get ideas for your story. Remember that a personal experience narrative (A Story About Me) has the following parts:

- a title that fits the story
- people you know, or events, special times, and memories that did or could have happened to you in real life
- a beginning, middle, and end (think about what happens first, next, then, and finally)

*Step*
**3**
Use the following prompt to complete the prewriting and writing activities:

> **Think about something that happened when you were younger. Choose a story that you remember or one you have heard from family or friends. Tell the story to a friend so that he or she can experience that memorable time.**

*Step*
**4**
Complete the graphic organizer for a personal experience narrative as your prewriting activity. Use your graphic organizer to help you think through your personal experience narrative.

*A full size graphic organizer can be found on page 22 of the Student Workbook.*

**PERSONAL EXPERIENCE NARRATIVE**

A Story About Me

Title: _____

| |
|---|
| Who was there? |
| Where did it happen? |
| When did it happen? |

| What Took Place? | First: |
|---|---|

| What Took Place? | Next: |
|---|---|

| What Took Place? | Then: |
|---|---|

| Finally: |
|---|

*Step* **5**

Use the information from your graphic organizer to complete your personal experience narrative. *(Students will have two pages to complete their writing activities.)*

### Writing Activity 4

_____

_____

_____

_____

*Step* **6**

The checklist shows what your best paper must have. Use the checklist below to review your work.

### Checklist for Writing Activity 4

☐ My story has a title.

☐ My story is about an experience that happened to me when I was younger.

☐ My story includes details about what happened.

☐ My story has a beginning, middle, and end.

☐ My personal experience narrative is well organized and complete.

☐ I try to spell words correctly.

☐ I use words that make my meaning clear. I do not use the same words over and over.

☐ I use correct punctuation and capitalization.

☐ I have written my story so that my reader can read my print or cursive writing.

## Additional Writing Prompts for a Fictional Narrative

1. You are living in another time, either the past or the future. Tell a story about an event that happens to you.

2. Tell a story about a character who is granted one wish. The character cannot wish for more wishes.

3. Something is missing. The main character in your story wakes up and finds that there is no electrical power, or gasoline, or clocks, or something that you choose on your own. Tell a story about how the main character's life changes.

4. Write a story about a character that has a super-human quality for one day. Describe something good that he or she made happen with the special ability.

5. Tell a story about a time when everyone looked alike.

## Additional Writing Prompts for a Personal Experience Narrative

**1.** Tell a story about a time when you lost something that was important to you. The item you lost could be a pet, a gift, a homework assignment, or anything else that is important to you.

**2.** Tell a story about a time you remember when the weather changed very quickly.

**3.** Tell a story about a wonderful teacher, coach, parent, relative, or friend whom you will never forget because of something he or she has done for you.

**4.** Write a personal experience narrative about the first time you did something by yourself. Describe a time that you didn't need any adult help such as riding your bike, preparing food, buying a gift, or baby-sitting.

**5.** You have earned some money. Tell a story about spending the money you earned.

**6.** Tell a story about a time when you were home alone, and you heard strange sounds.

# Chapter 2

# The Descriptive Communication Process
## (Journal and Letter)

## The Key Parts of this Chapter Include:

**1** Discussing the purpose and features of a letter and a journal.

**2** Showing how the descriptive communication process links to the eleven writing modes.

**3** Offering teaching tips on where students breakdown in the descriptive process.

**4** Providing ideas for the development of additional writing prompts for journals and letters.

---

The following teaching tools will be provided for a **journal** and a **letter**: graphic organizers, models, two writing prompts, and student checklists.

---

## What is the Descriptive Communication Process?

The purpose of description is to provide a visual picture of a person, place, or thing with vivid, written details. Two examples of the descriptive communication process are the journal and the letter. Journals have been used and defined in a variety of ways – writers' notebooks, dialogue journals, personal journals or diaries, learning logs, and project journals. Some ideas to help students generate thoughts for a journal include: memories, hobbies, current events, questions, pets, plans, hopes, discoveries, and personal news.

Letters must be written in the proper form: a greeting, body, and closing are included. Each letter will have a specific audience to address, however, an important thing to keep in mind is that the audience often varies from one letter to another.

Descriptions contain vivid sensory experiences and many specific details. The reader can imagine the person, place, or thing the writer describes. The written piece tells how the writer perceives the subject matter through as many senses as possible – sights, sounds, tastes, tactile sensations, and movement. A single person, place, or thing is often the major focal point for each descriptive section.

### Features of a Journal

- Often, the audience of a journal is oneself.
- The purpose of a journal is to record thoughts, feelings, and personal events.
- The format of a journal is often in paragraph form.
- The personal journal is often written in an informal style of writing.

> **Descriptive Communication information for students can be found on page 27 of the *Write on Target* Student Workbook.**

### Features of a Letter

- The audience of a letter is specific, and the purpose is often a personal communication.
- A letter clearly addresses the audience with the intent to communicate.
- A letter contains a greeting, body, and closing.
- A letter is written with a very specific purpose.

---

## Correlation of Descriptive Communication to the Writing Modes

Below are the writing modes that reflect the importance of the descriptive communication process. The ability to describe is embedded in virtually all writing tasks and formats and across all content areas. Good writers describe so readers can experience what the authors want their audiences to experience. The journal and the letter were selected as the formats for students to practice and refine their descriptive skills.

**Journal** – a piece of writing recounting the activities of a day, a month, or a year. Included within the journal should be the date, a description of the sights, sounds, people and events around the writer, and a description of the writer's feelings. Often, the audience for a journal is oneself. A journal may be written in letter or paragraph form.

**Letter** – a piece of writing, organized in the correct style of a letter (including a greeting, body, and closing), that addresses a specific audience with the intention of establishing a written connection or communication with them.

---

# Teaching Tips:
# Where Students Breakdown in the Descriptive Communication Process

• Students do not use sufficient details to recreate the picture.

• Students use unnecessary details to recreate the picture.

• Students have a tendency to shift into other modes, especially narrative.

• Students want to tell the reader what to think about the person, place, thing, or event, rather than showing the reader through vivid descriptions so the reader can form his or her own mental pictures. For example, a student may write, "*It took a long time,*" rather than, "*As I waited for the bell to ring, the hands on the clock never seemed to move.*"

• In letter formats, students often do not establish a personal connection with the reader. Students omit either opening or closing comments. Examples of acceptable comments are listed below.

**Sample opening comments:**

Hope all is well with you…

I hope this letter finds you well…

I enjoyed our last visit, or your last letter…

**Sample closing comments:**

I look forward to seeing you…

Hope to see you soon…

Please write and tell me more about…

# Writing Activity 5: Descriptive Journal

*Step*
*1*

Follow along as the November 12, 2000 journal entry is read.

**November 12, 2000**

Today was one of those days to remember. It was a day filled with life's simple pleasures. Awakening, I peeked out from under my soft comforter to realize I had time to spare before my alarm would go off. The house was so quiet, nothing like most mornings when I wake up late and rush around, getting dressed without a moment to spare.

As I leisurely proceeded to dress, the sounds of life in the room next to mine pierced the silence. A warm, mouthwatering aroma led me down to the kitchen, and there it was, a breakfast like no other: three pieces of golden French toast oozing with syrup next to crisp strips of bacon. A tall glass of apple juice sat glistening next to the plate. Mom stood over the stove flipping more French toast. She was so excited to have a day off; she celebrated by preparing a morning feast.

Turning the combination on my middle school locker, I remembered it was a special schedule day; there was no citizenship and no science. What a relief! And I could not believe my eyes when the cafeteria served pizza, my favorite, for lunch.

The special schedule meant fewer classes and no homework! When I got home, there was time to relax, talk on the phone, and chat online. Mom even let me stay up an hour later than usual.

After watching some TV, I headed for my "cave." I put on my favorite pajamas and sank into my mattress. I pulled my crisp, cool sheets and thick comforter around me and thought about the day.

I want to remember how great a day can be if I just enjoy the simple things. If I just appreciate the simple things, maybe every day can be a special one.

*Step* **2**
There are several things to keep in mind as you plan and write your journal entry. Remember, a good journal entry has the following parts:

- a date
- a description of the sights and sounds of the events or people
- a description of your feelings
- a beginning, middle, and end

*Step* **3**
Use the following prompt to complete the prewriting and writing activities:

> **You are thinking about someone who has made a difference in your life. In your journal, describe a special time you spent with this person so you will always remember this important time.**

*Step* **4**
Complete the graphic organizer for a journal as your prewriting activity. Use your graphic organizer to help you think through your journal entry.

*A full size graphic organizer can be found on page 30 of the Student Workbook.*

**JOURNAL**

What day will you write about in your journal?

Why are you writing about this day?

Describe the sights and sounds you remember from this day.

Who was there?

When and where did it happen?

| What Happened? | First: |
| What Happened? | Next: |
| What Happened? | Then: |

Finally:

How did what you're writing about make you and others feel?

**Step 5**

Use the information from your graphic organizer to complete your journal entry. *(Students will have two pages to complete their writing activities.)*

### Writing Activity 5

_____

_____

_____

_____

_____

**Step 6**

The checklist shows what your best paper must have. Use the checklist below to review your work.

### Checklist for Writing Activity 5

- ☐ My journal entry has a date.
- ☐ I describe a person who has made a difference in my life.
- ☐ I include details about how this person looks, sounds, and so on.
- ☐ I tell how this person made a difference in my life.
- ☐ My journal entry has a beginning, middle, and end.
- ☐ My journal entry is well organized and complete.
- ☐ I try to spell words correctly.
- ☐ I use words that make my meaning clear. I do not use the same words over and over.
- ☐ I use correct punctuation and capitalization.
- ☐ I have written my journal entry so the reader can read my print or cursive writing.

# Writing Activity 6: Descriptive Journal

*Step*
## 1

Follow along as the July 25, 2000 journal entry is read.

**July 25, 2000**

I wasn't sure I wanted to go on a family vacation to San Diego this year, but surprisingly, this trip has turned out to be an exciting experience. Today, we slept in, had a nice breakfast in the hotel restaurant, and took a carefree stroll, stopping in cool little shops along the way.

Our travels eventually led us to the site I had been waiting for: the Pacific Ocean. I'd seen pictures before, but it was hard to believe it could be so enormous. I stood there just looking out in amazement as the waves gently rolled in to touch the sand, then pulled back out again. The waves moved like this over and over. The sun was shining; it glistened on the water like hundreds of shiny diamonds. If only they were real, I would bottle them up, take them home, and sell them to the highest bidder. I could be rich!

Even though the diamonds were only figments of my imagination, the ocean was really neat. As I stood with my feet in the sand, I felt the warm breeze against my skin and breathed in the smell of salt water and fish from the harbor.

There were boats of every shape and size docked at the harbor's marina. I thought about all those boats used by so many different people for so many different purposes. Some people were using boats to sail and have fun. While others, like fishermen, used their boats to earn their livings. It was fun reading the boats' names. My favorite boat, a large, white sailboat with a blue stripe along the side, was named "The Sailing Samantha."

People who live in San Diego can see the ocean all the time. They probably don't realize how lucky they are to live close to such a great place. It makes me wonder if there are things I see every day around home that I take for granted. When we get back, I think I need to look at my surroundings in a whole new way. Maybe I'll even see a few diamonds I never noticed before.

*Step* **2**

There are several things to keep in mind as you plan and write your journal entry. Remember, a good journal entry has the following parts:

- a date
- a description of the sights and sounds of the people or events
- a description of your feelings
- a beginning, middle, and end

*Step* **3**

Use the following prompt to complete the prewriting and writing activities:

> **Think about the most important day of your life. Describe this day, or part of the day. What made this day so important? Include details so that others will know more about this memorable day.**

*Step* **4**

Complete the graphic organizer for a journal as your prewriting activity. Use your graphic organizer to help you think through your journal entry.

*A full size graphic organizer can be found on page 36 of the Student Workbook.*

### JOURNAL

What day will you write about in your journal?

Why are you writing about this day?

Describe the sights and sounds you remember from this day.

Who was there?

When and where did it happen?

| What Happened? | First: |
| What Happened? | Next: |
| What Happened? | Then: |

Finally:

How did what you're writing about make you and others feel?

*Step*
**5**
Use the information from your graphic organizer to complete your journal entry. *(Students will have two pages to complete their writing activities.)*

### Writing Activity 6

---

---

---

---

---

*Step*
**6**
The checklist shows what your best paper must have. Use the checklist below to review your work.

### Checklist for Writing Activity 6

- ☐ My journal entry has a date.

- ☐ I describe the most important day of my life in my journal entry.

- ☐ I include details about why this day is memorable.

- ☐ My journal entry has a beginning, middle, and end.

- ☐ My journal entry is well organized and complete.

- ☐ I try to spell words correctly.

- ☐ I use words that make my meaning clear. I do not use the same words over and over.

- ☐ I use correct punctuation and capitalization.

- ☐ I have written my journal entry so the reader can read my print or cursive writing.

# Writing Activity 7: Descriptive Letter

*Step*
**1**
Follow along as the descriptive letter below is read.

March 30, 2000

Dear Rachel,

Hi, how are you? I am having a great vacation with my family! I hope that you are having a good spring break, too. My family and I are staying with my grandparents at their house on Duck Key in Florida. We flew from Columbus, Ohio, to Miami, Florida, then drove nearly two hours over the Florida Keys to get to their house.

Grandma's and Grandpa's house faces the ocean, and they have a swimming pool with a diving board and a slide. My brother and I get up every morning and have relay races in the pool. So far, I am winning the most races.

Yesterday, my grandpa and I went to the beach. We fished off the pier, swam in the ocean, made a huge sandcastle, and collected seashells for my grandma. He even let me bury him in the sand! We also grilled hot dogs for lunch and sat under a big palm tree to relax.

Tonight we are going out to a restaurant to celebrate Grandma's birthday. Grandma wants me to try the crab legs for dinner. I'm not sure I will like the taste of crab legs, but I'm sure I will enjoy a slice of Grandma's birthday cake!

We will be leaving here on Saturday. I hate to see this vacation end, but I do miss you and all of our friends. I will see you at school on Monday.

Your friend,

Anita

*Step* **2**
There are several things to keep in mind as you plan and write your descriptive letter. Remember, a good descriptive letter has the following parts:

- a date
- a greeting
- a body that talks to the reader
- a closing
- a signature

*Step* **3**
Use the following prompt to complete the prewriting and writing activities:

**Write a letter to someone who is older than you. Write about what it is like growing up in your time. You might include information such as the style of clothes you wear, the music you listen to, and the types of things that interest you.**

*Step* **4**
Complete the graphic organizer for a descriptive letter as your prewriting activity. Use your graphic organizer to help you think through your descriptive letter.

*A full size graphic organizer can be found on page 42 of the Student Workbook.*

**DESCRIPTIVE LETTER**

Date:

Greeting:

Personal comment and why you are writing:

**Details**

First:

Second:

Third:

Fourth:

Personal comments ending the letter:

Closing:

Signature:

*Step*
**5**
Use the information from your graphic organizer to complete your letter.
*(Students will have two pages to complete their writing activities.)*

## Writing Activity 7

_____

_____

_____

_____

*Step*
**6**
The checklist shows what your best paper must have. Use the checklist below to review your work.

## Checklist for Writing Activity 7

❑ I use the form for a letter with a date, a greeting, a body, a closing, and a signature.

❑ My letter tells my reader why I am writing and makes personal comments.

❑ My letter describes what it's like to grow up in my time.

❑ My letter is well organized and complete.

❑ My descriptive letter includes a personal closing comment.

❑ I try to spell words correctly.

❑ I use words that make my meaning clear. I do not use the same words over and over.

❑ I use correct punctuation and capitalization.

❑ I have written my letter so the reader can read my print or cursive writing.

# Writing Activity 8: Descriptive Letter

*Step*

*1* Follow along as the descriptive letter below is read.

July 12, 2000

Dear Mom and Dad,

Hello, how are you? Summer camp is really cool! We are staying in a cabin with a large room that sleeps eight boys. The cabin is made of large pine logs with a tin roof. There are large screen windows on three sides of the cabin and shutters attached to each window to close if it rains. A bunk bed is placed in each corner of the room. Ryan and I are sharing a bunk. I sleep on the top bunk because Ryan is afraid that he will forget where he is sleeping and fall out of bed at night. Showers and restrooms are a short walk away.

The food here is pretty good. For every meal, the cabins take turns serving. Yesterday, it was our turn to serve breakfast. I served blueberry pancakes, Ryan dished out cups of fruit, J.P. was in charge of bacon, and Kyle poured the juice. Bill, Darius, Andre, and Levi cleared the plates from the tables and helped with the dishes.

My counselor's name is Mike, and he's very nice. He is a college junior from Missouri. He showed us how to make s'mores last night. You melt a marshmallow and place it on a piece of a chocolate bar, then sandwich the marshmallow and chocolate between graham crackers.

We have been swimming, fishing, and canoeing on the lake every day. The water was cold at first, but I got used to it. The girls from across the lake are coming over tomorrow night for a cook-out and games. We are going to play Capture the Flag. Our cabin has a plan to beat them. Can't wait to see you Sunday!

Love,

Oliver

*Step*
**2**

There are several things to keep in mind as you plan and write your descriptive letter. Remember, a good descriptive letter has the following parts:

- a date
- a greeting
- a body that talks to the reader
- a closing
- a signature

*Step*
**3**

Use the following prompt to complete the prewriting and writing activities:

**Write a letter to a person of your choice describing your favorite place. In your letter, include why the person you are writing to would enjoy visiting your favorite place.**

*Step*
**4**

Complete the graphic organizer for a descriptive letter as your prewriting activity. Use your graphic organizer to help you think through your descriptive letter.

*A full size graphic organizer can be found on page 48 of the Student Workbook.*

**DESCRIPTIVE LETTER**

Date:

Greeting:

Personal comment and why you are writing:

**Details**

First:

Second:

Third:

Fourth:

Personal comments ending the letter:

Closing:

Signature:

*Step*

**5**

Use the information from your graphic organizer to complete your letter. *(Students will have two pages to complete their writing activities.)*

### Writing Activity 8

_____

_____

_____

_____

*Step*

**6**

The checklist shows what your best paper must have. Use the checklist below to review your work.

### Checklist for Writing Activity 8

☐ I use the form for a letter with a date, a greeting, a body, a closing, and a signature.

☐ My letter tells my reader why I am writing and makes personal comments.

☐ My letter describes my favorite place.

☐ I include why the person I am writing to would like to visit my favorite place.

☐ My descriptive letter includes a personal closing comment.

☐ I try to spell words correctly.

☐ I use words that make my meaning clear. I do not use the same words over and over.

☐ I use correct punctuation and capitalization.

☐ I have written my letter so the reader can read my print or cursive writing.

## Additional Writing Prompts for a Journal Entry

1. Describe something that makes you thankful.

2. Describe someone you consider to be a true friend.

3. Describe yourself and something you do well.

4. Describe a goal you have for the future. One example might be to describe what you want to be when you grow up.

5. Describe yourself after you have stayed up most of the night.

6. Describe one of your "firsts": your first plane ride, a new food you tried, a new place you visited, a friend you just met.

## Additional Writing Prompts for a Descriptive Letter

1. The KDC radio station is offering a free trip for the best letter describing where you want to visit and why. Write the letter so you will win the trip.

2. Write a letter to a friend describing your most embarrassing moment.

3. Write a letter to someone describing a gift you would like to receive for a special occasion.

4. Write a letter to a family member about something you have successfully accomplished.

# Chapter 3

# The Direction Communication Process
## (Directions and Invitation)

## The Key Parts of this Chapter Include:

**1** Discussing the purpose and features of directions and an invitation.

**2** Showing how the direction communication process links to the eleven writing modes.

**3** Offering teaching tips on where students breakdown in the direction process.

**4** Providing ideas for the development of additional writing prompts for directions and an invitation.

---

The following teaching tools are provided for sets of **directions** and an **invitation**: graphic organizers, models, two writing prompts, and student checklists.

---

## What is the Direction Communication Process?

The purpose of the direction communication process is to provide a set of actions that lead to a goal such as going somewhere or making something. Two examples of the direction communication process are directions and an invitation.

### Features of Directions

- Directions provide communication that is orderly and efficient.
- Directions assume the person that is being directed is not familiar with the task.
- Directions are written in correct chronological order or consecutive order.

> **Direction Communication information for students can be found on page 53 of the *Write on Target* Student Workbook.**

### Words that Provide Directions

- direction words: right, left, north, south, east, west
- prepositions: in, on, under, before, after
- adverbial phrases: when you see the… before you reach the… after you pass the…
- direction verbs: mix, blend, stir, insert, pour

### Features of an Invitation
- An invitation tells who is invited, and who is hosting the event.
- An invitation indicates the type of event.
- An invitation indicates the time and date of the event.
- An invitation indicates where the event will take place and often includes a map to the location.

## Correlation of Direction Communication to the Writing Modes

**Directions** – a piece of writing explaining how to do something (e.g., how to go somewhere, or how to make something). Using step-by-step order, the directions should clearly describe the materials that are necessary to complete the task. It may be written in paragraph form or line by line, but must include a starting point and an ending point.

**Invitation** – a piece of writing, possibly in the form of a letter, that includes the following information: the purpose of the invitation, who is writing the invitation, who is being invited, where they are being invited to, when they are being invited, and any other important information.

## Teaching Tips:
## Where Students Breakdown in the Direction Communication Process

- Students leave out information important to the completion of the task or goal because they assume the readers know what the students know.

- Students provide more information than is necessary for the efficient completion of the task — they distract the readers with too much information.

- Students do not understand or do not use "direction words."

- Students tend to switch into other communication modes, especially narrative.

# Writing Activity 9: Directions (How to Do Something)

*Step* Follow along as the directions on how to make a banana split are read.

*1*

## How To Make A Banana Split

A banana split is a great dessert that's easy to make. Banana splits require the following ingredients: bananas, ice cream, hot fudge or chocolate sauce, whipped cream, chopped peanuts, and cherries. You will also need boat-shaped dishes, an ice cream spoon, a dull knife, and serving spoons.

1. The first and most important ingredient in a banana split is the banana. Start by peeling a banana. Then, using a dull knife, carefully slice the banana lengthwise so you have two canoe shaped slices.

2. Place the banana slices in a boat-shaped dish or any dish that is long enough to hold the slices. If you don't have a long dish, cut each banana slice in half and place all four pieces in a bowl.

3. Next, you will need your ice cream. Most people prefer vanilla ice cream on their banana splits, but you can serve any flavor you like. Scoop out two spoonfuls of ice cream and place them side-by-side on your bananas.

4. Now it is time for the hot fudge or chocolate sauce. Pour as much as you would like all over the banana slices and scoops of ice cream.

5. At this time, sprinkle three spoonfuls of peanuts onto the banana split. If you have any other favorite toppings you would like to enjoy on your dessert, add them now.

Finally, put some whipped cream on each scoop of ice cream, and top off your delicious banana split with two cherries. Serve the banana split to a friend, or enjoy this wonderful dessert by yourself.

*Step*
2

There are several things to keep in mind as you plan and write your directions. Remember, good directions have the following parts:

- a beginning that tells what the directions will explain how to do
- a description of what is needed to complete the task
- steps are given in order (directions may be written line by line or in paragraph form)
- a starting and ending point are included
- begin your directions with an opening statement and end with a concluding sentence

*Step*
3

Use the following prompt to complete the prewriting and writing activities:

> **A friend has asked you how to make your favorite food. Write a set of directions to make your favorite food so your friend can follow them easily. Once your directions are written, have your friend follow them exactly.**

*Step*
4

Complete the graphic organizer for directions on how to do something as your prewriting activity. Use your graphic organizer to help you think through your directions.

*A full size graphic organizer can be found on page 56 of the Student Workbook.*

**DIRECTIONS**
How To Do Something

How To: _____

What is needed to begin...

Step 1:

Step 2:

Step 3:

Step 4:

Step 5:

Finally:

**Step 5**

Use the information from your graphic organizer to complete your directions. *(Students will have two pages to complete their writing activities.)*

### Writing Activity 9

_____

_____

_____

_____

**Step 6**

The checklist shows what your best paper must have. Use the checklist below to review your work.

### Checklist for Writing Activity 9

☐ My directions begin with a sentence telling what my directions will explain how to do.

☐ My directions clearly describe the materials that are needed to make my favorite food.

☐ My directions use the correct order to tell my friend what to do first, next, and so on, to make my favorite food.

☐ My directions have a concluding sentence describing my favorite food.

☐ My directions are well organized and complete.

☐ I try to spell words correctly.

☐ I use words that make my meaning clear. I do not use the same words over and over.

☐ I use correct punctuation and capitalization.

☐ I have written my directions so the reader can read my print or cursive writing.

# Writing Activity 10: Directions (How to Go Somewhere)

*Step*
*1*

Look at the map below. Follow along as the set of directions for traveling from the Food Court to the Theater Parking Lot is read to you.

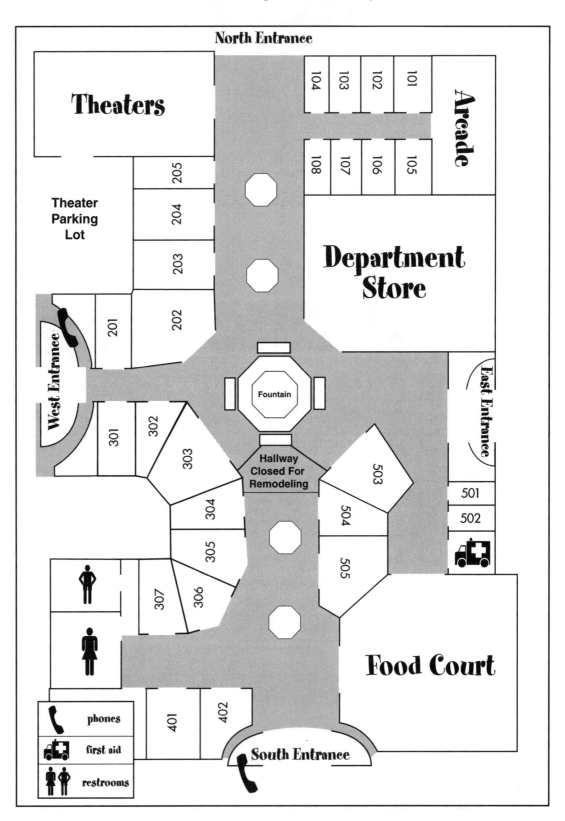

*Step*

*1*

## Directions for Traveling from the Food Court to the Theater Parking Lot

You are located in the Food Court in the southeast corner of the mall. You are trying to get to the Theater Parking Lot found south of the Theaters.

1. Exit the Food Court to the north until you see the east entrance of the mall.

2. Walk west toward the fountain.

3. Travel around the fountain in the northwest direction. Do not pass the north entrance mall hallway.

4. Head toward the north entrance. You will see the Theaters at the end of the hall, on the west side.

5. Go through the theaters toward the southern exit.

You have made it to the Theater Parking Lot.

*Step*

*2*

There are several things to keep in mind as you plan and write your own directions. Remember, good directions have the following parts:

- a beginning that tells where the directions begin and end
- a description of what is needed to complete the task
- steps are given in order
- a starting and ending point are included

*Step*

# 3

Use the following prompt to complete the prewriting and writing activities:

You and a good friend are playing "Monster Man" at the Arcade. You look at your watch and realize the movie you planned to see has already started. Your friend volunteers to call his parents and let them know you need to be picked up early. You remember seeing a sign that says the phones at the West Entrance are out of order. Using the map of the mall, give directions to your friend on how to get to the phones at the South Entrance of the mall.

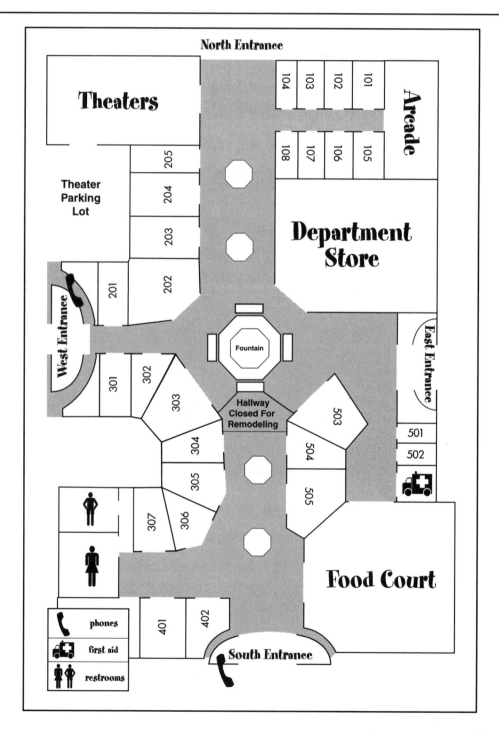

*Step*
## 4

Using the map of the mall, complete the graphic organizer for directions on how to go somewhere as your prewriting activity. Use your graphic organizer to help you think through your directions.

*A full size graphic organizer can be found on page 64 of the Student Workbook.*

**DIRECTIONS**
**How To Go Somewhere**

**Where are you going?**

**Where to start...**

**First:**

**Second:**

**Third:**

**Fourth:**

**Fifth:**

**Where you finish...**

*Step*
## 5

Use the information from the map and your graphic organizer to complete your directions. *(Students will have two pages to complete their writing activities.)*

**Writing Activity 10**

*Step*

6

The checklist shows what your best paper must have. Use the checklist below to review your work.

## Checklist for Writing Activity 10

☐ My directions start with a sentence telling where my directions begin and end.

☐ My directions use step-by-step order (1,2,3,4…) to tell my friend what to do first, next, and so on, in order to walk from the Arcade to the phone booth at the South Entrance.

☐ My directions give accurate details and directions.

☐ My directions include a concluding sentence.

☐ My directions are well organized and complete.

☐ I try to spell words correctly.

☐ I use words that make my meaning clear. I do not use the same words over and over.

☐ I use correct punctuation and capitalization.

☐ I have written my directions so the reader can read my print or cursive writing.

# Writing Activity 11: Invitation

**Step** Follow along as the invitation below is read.

**1**

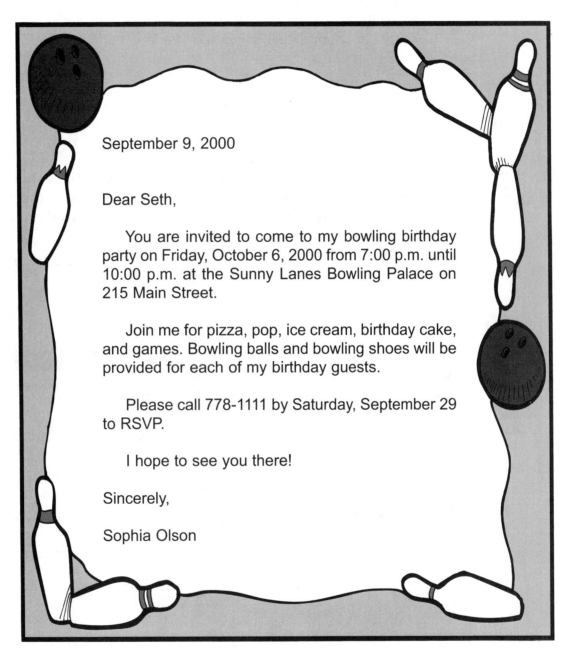

September 9, 2000

Dear Seth,

You are invited to come to my bowling birthday party on Friday, October 6, 2000 from 7:00 p.m. until 10:00 p.m. at the Sunny Lanes Bowling Palace on 215 Main Street.

Join me for pizza, pop, ice cream, birthday cake, and games. Bowling balls and bowling shoes will be provided for each of my birthday guests.

Please call 778-1111 by Saturday, September 29 to RSVP.

I hope to see you there!

Sincerely,

Sophia Olson

*Step* **2**

There are several things to keep in mind as you plan and write your invitation. Remember, a good invitation has the following parts:

- provides information about where and when to attend
- includes the purpose of the event
- provides information for an RSVP
- gives all important details about the event

*Step* **3**

Use the following prompt to complete the prewriting and writing activities:

> **Write an invitation to parents of students in your class. Invite the parents to participate in your school's career day. Ask them to come and present information about their careers to the members of your class.**

*Step* **4**

Complete the graphic organizer for an invitation as your prewriting activity. Use your graphic organizer to help you think through your invitation.

*A full size graphic organizer can be found on page 70 of the Student Workbook.*

### INVITATION

What is the invitation for?

Who is writing the invitation?

Who is being invited?

Where? (location)

When? (date and time)

Other important information:

R.S.V.P. (who and when)

**Step 5** Use the information from your graphic organizer to complete your invitation. *(Students will have two pages to complete their writing activities.)*

### Writing Activity 11

_____

_____

_____

_____

**Step 6** The checklist shows what your best paper must have. Use the checklist below to review your work.

### Checklist for Writing Activity 11

☐ My invitation includes all the important details for my classmates' parents such as where and when to attend, and RSVP information.

☐ I let my classmates' parents know why I am inviting them.

☐ My invitation is well organized and complete.

☐ I try to spell words correctly.

☐ I use words that make my meaning clear. I do not use the same words over and over.

☐ I use correct punctuation and capitalization.

☐ I have written my invitation so the reader can read my print or cursive writing.

# Writing Activity 12: Invitation

*Step* Follow along as the invitation below is read.

*1*

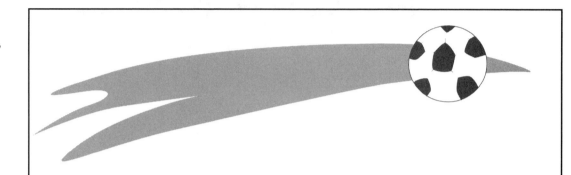

August 2, 2000

Dear Rocket Soccer Player,

The end of the season is coming soon! In order to celebrate the great season we had this fall, I would like to invite you and your family to an end of the season cookout and pool party on Friday, August 20, 2000. Please come around 1:30 p.m. You are welcome to stay as long as you would like.

Awards for the season will be given at 2:30 p.m. There will be hot dogs and hamburgers on the grill, as well as pasta salad, chips, and pop. Don't forget your bathing suit and towel for swimming after the awards.

The party will be held at my house at 1222 Eastgate Drive. To RSVP, please call me at 987-2222 before August 15, 2000.

Sincerely,

Coach Baker

*Step*

**2**

There are several things to keep in mind as you plan and write your invitation. Remember, a good invitation has the following parts:

- provides information about where and when to attend
- includes the purpose of the event
- provides information for an RSVP
- gives all important details about the event

*Step*

**3**

Use the following prompt to complete the prewriting and writing activities:

**Write an invitation to your friends inviting them to a picnic to celebrate the end of the school year.**

*Step*

**4**

Complete the graphic organizer for an invitation as your prewriting activity. Use your graphic organizer to help you think through your invitation.

*A full size graphic organizer can be found on page 76 of the Student Workbook.*

### INVITATION

**What is the invitation for?**

**Who is writing the invitation?**

**Who is being invited?**

**Where? (location)**

**When? (date and time)**

**Other important information:**

**R.S.V.P. (who and when)**

*Step*
5

Use the information from your graphic organizer to complete your invitation. *(Students will have two pages to complete their writing activities.)*

### Writing Activity 12

_____

_____

_____

_____

*Step*
6

The checklist shows what your best paper must have. Use the checklist below to review your work.

### Checklist for Writing Activity 12

❏ My invitation includes all the important details for my guests such as where and when to attend, and RSVP information.

❏ I let my guests know why I am inviting them.

❏ I try to spell words correctly.

❏ I use interesting words.

❏ My sentences and proper names begin with a capital letter.

❏ My sentences end with a period, an exclamation point, or a question mark.

❏ I have written my invitation so the reader can read my print or cursive writing.

## Additional Writing Prompts for Directions on How to Do Something

1. how to pack an overnight bag

2. how to clean your room

3. how to wash your hands

4. how to set the dinner table

5. how to wash your hair

6. Teach an adult who does not know much about electronic equipment to use a new technology. The technology could include a VCR, a DVD player, a CD player, or anything with which you are familiar.

## Additional Writing Prompts for Directions on How to Go Somewhere or How to Find Something

1. Using a map of the United States, have students write directions for traveling from one location to another.

2. Using a state map, have students write directions for traveling from one location to another.

3. Using a local map, have students write directions for traveling from one location to another.

4. Using a globe or map of the world, have students write directions for traveling from one location to another.

5. Using a map of a store, amusement park, museum, or library, have students write directions for traveling from one location to another.

**Additional Writing Prompts for Writing an Invitation to:**

1. a class presentation.

2. a special lunch.

3. a play or musical production.

4. a concert.

5. a sporting event.

6. a competition in which you are participating.

# Chapter 4

# The Explanation Communication Process
## (Informational Report, Summary, and Thank-You Note)

## The Key Parts of this Chapter Include:

**1** Discussing the purpose and features of an informational report, a summary, and a thank-you note.

**2** Showing how the explanation communication process links to the eleven writing modes.

**3** Providing teaching tips on where students breakdown during the explanation process.

**4** Providing ideas for the development of additional writing prompts for an informational report, a summary, and a thank-you note.

---

The following teaching tools will be provided for an **informational report**, a **summary**, and a **thank-you note**: graphic organizers, models, two writing prompts, and student checklists.

---

## What is the Explanation Communication Process?

Explanation is a communication process that appears across all subject areas in the curriculum. The purpose of explanation is for the writer to give reasons why something occurred.

For an explanation, the writer gives a reason or an opinion with a justification; he or she must be able to provide facts with supporting details. An explanation may require the ability to infer (i.e., Why do you think the character felt that way?). Oftentimes, an explanation requires the ability to use only information given in a selection to support the explanation (i.e., Use information from the selection to support your answer.). Understanding cause and effect is important to the explanation process (i.e., This____ happened because...).

### Features of an Informational Report
- An informational report is nonfiction writing about a person, place, thing, or event.
- An informational report provides information about some or all of the following questions:

What or who is it?          Where is it?
What does it look like?      When is it?
What does it do?            Why is it important?

### Features of a Summary (Only the Important Information)
- The main idea is identified in a summary.
- Supporting details are not included in a summary.
- Trivial and redundant information is not included in a summary.
- Similar facts, ideas, and information are grouped across paragraphs.
- A summary conveys only the information essential to complete the communication.
- The summary is shorter in length than the original.
- A summary is told in the student's own words.

> Explanation Communication information for students can be found on page 81 of the *Write on Target* Student Workbook.

### Features of the Thank-You Note
- A thank-you not is written in letter format with greeting, body, and closing.
- A thank-you note explains why the writer is thankful for something done for, or given to, him or her.

---

## Correlation of Explanation Communication to the Writing Modes

**Informational** – a piece of nonfiction writing based upon researched facts. Its purpose is to inform the audience about a topic (the topic can cover a wide variety of subjects) the author has learned about. This mode of writing is presented in an organized format consisting of a beginning, middle, and end, and is written in the student's own words.

**Summary** – a piece of writing that identifies what the text selection is about and states the main ideas of the text selection. It does not include information that is not important, and has fewer details than a retelling.

**Thank-You Note** – a piece of writing in the form of a letter, including a greeting, body and closing, that explains what the writer is thankful for and why.

# Teaching Tips:
# Where Students Breakdown in the Explanation Communication Process

## In general, students have difficulty:
- understanding when to infer and when to use the selection to make their points. (Example: Students are asked to use ONLY the text selection to provide evidence for their opinions or statements....or students are asked to explain their own opinions, conclusions, or observations based on the information provided in the text.)
- understanding the relationship between cause and effect.
- using facts and supporting details.
- distinguishing between facts and opinions in the selection.

## Informational Report
- Students have difficulty organizing the information in a logical order.
- Student writers do not provide closings to their reports. The closing should summarize the importance of the ideas presented.
- Some students are unable to pick out the important ideas and eliminate nonessential information.
- Some students have difficulty writing the ideas in their own words.

## Summary
- Students have difficulty picking out the main idea, especially in paragraphs that do not have topic sentences.
- Students have difficulty eliminating nonessential information.
- Students have difficulty using titles, subheadings, and boldface words to compose their summaries.

## Thank-You Note
- Students do not address the reader with an appropriate greeting.
- Students have difficulty explaining or expressing why the gift or favor was appreciated.

# Writing Activity 13: Informational Report

*Step* 1   Follow along as the informational report "The First Surfers" is read.

## The First Surfers

Although no one can be absolutely sure about the origins of surfing, as early as the twelfth century, surfers carved pictures of their traditions into Hawaiian lava rock.

The origin of surfing is deeply rooted in the ancient Hawaiian system of laws, which favored royalty over commoners in the kingdom. Hawaiians referred to surfing as "he'enalu" or wave sliding. He'enalu was a noble and exclusive occupation for kings and queens. Chiefs used wave sliding and other sports to show their strength and command over their people. The great skill the royal surfers displayed led people to believe the surf riders were supreme over both water and land.

Although surfing was very important to the Hawaiian culture in the late 1700s, the sport was deeply affected by the arrival of Europeans and Americans who came first as explorers and traders and later as missionaries and settlers. Missionaries described surfing as dangerous, disorganized, terrifying, and confusing. Declaring the sport a waste of time, they preached against surfing and introduced Hawaiians to new forms of recreation. By 1890, surfing in Hawaii was nearly extinct. If not for the dedication of a few kings, surfing may not have survived.

By the early 1900s, the missionaries' influence in Hawaii began to decline. In 1905, a teenager named Duke Kahanamoku, who spent most of his days surfing, formed a surf club with his friends, "The Club of Waves." Duke's club was credited with getting Hawaiians excited about surfing again.

The popularity of surfing eventually made its way to the California coast in the 1950s. The waves along the shoreline, the introduction of lighter weight surfboards made of polyester foam or fiberglass, teen surf movies, beach parties, and popular music all helped to renew people's interest in surfing. Surfing remains a popular sport today, particularly in Hawaii, California, and Australia.

*Step*
*2*

There are several things to keep in mind as you plan and write your own informational report. Remember, a good informational report includes the following parts:

- a title
- tells what your report is about
- includes only important information
- tells what you have learned

*Step*
*3*

Use the following prompt to complete the prewriting and writing activities:

**Read through the information given about tornadoes on the next page. Use the Information Planning Guide to select and group the information you will use to create paragraphs that provide the reader with information about tornadoes. Use the information you gather in the planning guide to complete your graphic organizer. You do not have to use every fact to complete your report. You will need to organize the material and add words of your own.**

**Write a report on tornadoes. Use the facts given, or add facts that you know. Use the informational report organizer to write an introduction, a body of one to three paragraphs, and a summary that ends your report.**

*Step*
# 3

## Tornado Facts & Safety

- Crouch down and cover your head.
- The largest tornadoes, classified as F4 or F5, can be more than one mile wide, last up to an hour or more, and travel over paths averaging 30-35 miles long.
- If you are outside during a tornado, go to the basement of a nearby building or lie flat in a ditch.
- The rotating winds of tornadoes may range from about 40 miles per hour to more than 300 miles per hour.
- A tornado often looks like a funnel with the fat part at the top.
- The Fujita Scale, developed by Theodore Fujita, a University of Chicago scientist, is used to classify tornadoes.
- A tornado watch means a tornado is possible.
- If you are in a car or mobile home, get out and head for safety.
- Tornadoes can occur in most parts of the world, except in polar regions.
- Meteorologists can predict possible severe weather 12 to 48 hours in advance.
- If there is a tornado warning, go inside to a safe place to protect yourself from flying glass or debris.
- Tornadoes are sometimes called "twisters."
- F0 and F1 tornadoes are the smallest and weakest.
- A tornado is a violent column of air extending from a thunderstorm to the ground.
- Tornadoes can be various sizes, shapes, and colors.
- The Red Cross suggests you assemble a disaster supplies kit that includes a first aid kit, a battery powered radio, a flashlight and extra batteries, bottled water, nonperishable food, a can opener, sturdy shoes, work gloves, and instructions on how to turn off home utilities.
- A tornado warning means a tornado has been spotted.
- Tornadoes most often hit the midwestern and southern United States during the spring and summer months.
- After a tornado, watch out for fallen power lines.
- Tornadoes are classified by wind speed and damage, according to the Fujita Scale.
- The National Weather Service is locating Doppler radar units across the country to detect air movement.
- Signs of a tornado may include: a greenish-black color to the sky, falling hail, the sound of a railroad train, and a funnel shaped cloud.
- Never use candles during a tornado.
- Go to interior rooms or halls on the lowest floor.
- Before a tornado, purchase a weather radio with a warning alarm tone and battery back-up to receive warnings.

*Step*
*4*
Complete the information planning guide and the graphic organizer for an informational report as your prewriting activities. Use your planning guide and graphic organizer to help you think through your informational report.

*A full size Information Planning Guide can be found on page 85 of the Student Workbook.*

*A full size graphic organizer can be found on page 86 of the Student Workbook.*

**Information Planning Guide**

Topic:

| Planning Questions (use questions that apply) | Key Words – Short Notes |
|---|---|
| What are they? | |
| What do they do? | |
| What do they look like? | |
| Where are they found? | |
| Why are they important? | |
| Summary – What are the most important things you have learned about this topic? | |

**INFORMATIONAL REPORT**

Title: _____

**INTRODUCTION (What is the report about?)**

**Paragraph 1:**

**Paragraph 2:**

**Paragraph 3:**

**SUMMARY (The most important points you want to make.)**

*Step* **5** Use the information from your graphic organizer to complete your informational report. (*Students will have two pages to complete their writing activities.*)

### Writing Activity 13

_____

_____

_____

_____

*Step* **6** The checklist shows what your best paper must have. Use the checklist below to review your work.

### Checklist for Writing Activity 13

- ☐ My informational report has a title.
- ☐ My informational report tells the reader what my report is about.
- ☐ My report includes only points that are important for readers to know.
- ☐ My report does not include information that is not important to make my points.
- ☐ My report tells the reader what I have learned.
- ☐ My report has a beginning, middle, and end.
- ☐ My report is well organized and complete.
- ☐ I try to spell words correctly without using any help.
- ☐ I use words that make my meaning clear. I do not use the same words over and over.
- ☐ I use correct punctuation and capitalization.

# Writing Activity 14: Informational Report

*Step*
**1**
Follow along as the informational report "Cesar Estrada Chavez" is read.

## Cesar Estrada Chavez

Cesar Estrada Chavez, the grandson of Mexican immigrants, was born March 31, 1927, near Yuma, Arizona. In the late 1930s, Cesar and his family moved to California where they became part of the migrant community that traveled from farm to farm, community to community, picking fruits and vegetables during harvest times. Living conditions were poor for the farm workers; the days were long and the pay was small. The Chavez family often found themselves sleeping in their car.

Once Cesar completed the eighth grade, he quit school and worked full-time in the vineyards. Cesar joined the Navy in 1944 and served for two years, fighting in World War II. After completing his military duty, he moved back to California and returned to work in the fields. Cesar began to see a need for change. In 1948, he took part in an unsuccessful strike to protest low wages and poor working conditions. By 1952, Cesar was traveling throughout California, making speeches in support of farm workers' rights and urging Mexican-Americans to register to vote.

Cesar led a successful strike of California grape-pickers in 1965 that lasted for five years. The striking workers demanded higher wages and encouraged Americans to boycott grapes. The strike attracted national attention, and for the first time, increased public awareness of the terrible conditions farm workers faced. Chavez was able to rally millions of supporters for the farm workers' cause.

Throughout his lifetime, Cesar continued to fight for farm workers' rights. He also fought against the use of toxic pesticides on grapes and other produce. Cesar advocated nonviolent protest and became well respected throughout the country. Cesar E. Chavez died on April 23, 1993, but his legacy of establishing farm workers' rights continues, today.

*Step*
**2**

There are several things to keep in mind as you plan and write your own informational report. Remember, a good informational report includes the following parts:

- a title
- tells what your report is about
- includes only important information
- tells what you have learned

*Step*
**3**

Use the following prompt to complete the prewriting and writing activities:

**Read through the information given about the Underground Railroad on the next page. Use the Information Planning Guide to select and group the information you will use to create paragraphs that provide the reader with information about the Underground Railroad. Use the information you gather in the planning guide to complete your graphic organizer. You do not have to use every fact to complete your report. You will need to organize the material and add words of your own.**

**Write a report on the Underground Railroad. Use the facts given, or add facts that you know. Use the informational report organizer to write an introduction, a body of one to three paragraphs, and a summary that ends your report.**

*Step*
# 3

## Facts About the Underground Railroad

- The Underground Railroad wasn't a railroad at all.
- The Underground Railroad was a network of anti-slavery Northerners who provided food, shelter, and a safe place for slaves seeking freedom.
- The purpose of the Underground Railroad was to help slaves reach safety in free states or in Canada.
- Runaway slaves used the North Star to guide their way.
- Slaves who escaped looked for "stations" in towns where free blacks and others would help hide them.
- "Conductors" met runaways at border points, such as Cincinnati, Ohio.
- Harriet Tubman was a famous "conductor" who was nicknamed "Moses."
- The runaways faced dangers of being captured by bloodhounds or patrollers.
- Handbills would often advertise the escape of a slave.
- Runaways would travel at night, often following rivers and staying off roads.
- Some historians believe the Underground Railroad helped make people aware of the evils of slavery.
- "A friend with friends" was a password used by conductors.
- With the passage of the Fugitive Slave Law of 1850, runaway slaves were not safe in northern cities. The law stated that a person could be fined or imprisoned for not helping a federal marshal arrest a runaway.
- The Society of Friends, or Quakers, actively fought for the rights of runaways.
- A lantern on a hitching post would signal a "safe house."
- A good friend of Harriet Tubman was the Quaker businessman Thomas Garrett. Garrett worked the Underground Railroad for over 40 years.
- The routes to freedom were often over 500 miles long.
- For some runaways, the journey to Canada took from two months to one year.
- Often, runaways would be forced to hide in wood boxes, secret passageways, or even specially designed cupboards.
- In 1865, slavery was abolished with the 13th Amendment to the United States Constitution.

*Step*

*4*

Complete the information planning guide and the graphic organizer for an informational report as your prewriting activities. Use your planning guide and graphic organizer to help you think through your informational report.

*A full size Information Planning Guide can be found on page 93 of the Student Workbook.*

*A full size graphic organizer can be found on page 94 of the Student Workbook.*

**Information Planning Guide**

Topic:

| Planning Questions (use questions that apply) | Key Words – Short Notes |
|---|---|
| What are they? | |
| What do they do? | |
| What do they look like? | |
| Where are they found? | |
| Why are they important? | |
| Summary – What are the most important things you have learned about this topic? | |

**INFORMATIONAL REPORT**

Title: _____

INTRODUCTION (What is the report about?)

Paragraph 1:

Paragraph 2:

Paragraph 3:

SUMMARY (The most important points you want to make.)

***Step* 5**  Use the information from your graphic organizer to complete your informational report. (*Students will have two pages to complete their writing activities.*)

**Writing Activity 14**

_____

_____

_____

_____

***Step* 6**  The checklist shows what your best paper must have. Use the checklist below to review your work.

**Checklist for Writing Activity 14**

❑ My informational report has a title.

❑ My informational report tells the reader what my report is about.

❑ My report includes only points that are important for readers to know.

❑ My report does not include information that is not important to make my points.

❑ My report tells the reader what I have learned.

❑ My report has a beginning, middle, and end.

❑ My report is well organized and complete.

❑ I try to spell words correctly without using any help.

❑ I use words that make my meaning clear. I do not use the same words over and over.

❑ I use correct punctuation and capitalization.

# Writing Activity 15: Summary

*Step*
*1*

Follow along as two passages are read aloud. The first passage is titled "The New Golden Dollar." The second passage is a summary of "The New Golden Dollar."

---

## The New Golden Dollar

Many Americans wonder what's the story behind the new Golden Dollar. In the early 1990s, the demand for dollar coins surged as the vending machine industry began to recognize the benefits of dollar coins. This increased demand began to exhaust the government's supply of Susan B. Anthony one-dollar coins.

On December 1, 1997, President Bill Clinton signed into law the "United States Dollar Coin Act of 1997," requiring the U.S. Treasury Department to place into circulation a new one-dollar coin. The new Golden Dollar would replace the Susan B. Anthony coin, that had been in circulation since 1979. According to the Coin Act, the new dollar coin had to meet several requirements. The coin had to be gold in color and have the same diameter as the Susan B. Anthony coin: 26.5 millimeters. Its edge needed to be smooth. The coin had to have metallic, anti-counterfeiting properties similar to other U.S. coins. The obverse side of the new coin had to show one or more women; the coin could not picture a living person. The reverse side had to display an eagle.

Once the requirements were issued, the next step was deciding who would be featured on the obverse side of the coin. In April 1998, the Dollar Coin Design Advisory Committee was formed. The committee met in open session and took suggestions from the public. Ideas for the coin's design came by mail and e-mail, through faxes, and phone messages.

On June 9, 1998, the design committee recommended the new Golden Dollar coin feature Sacagawea, the Native American woman who assisted Lewis and Clark on their expedition from the Northern Great Plains to the Pacific Ocean. Once the recommendation was accepted, the U.S. Mint contacted individuals and organizations to submit coin designs. Almost one year and 121 designs later, the final design for the Golden Dollar was revealed on May 4, 1999. Full-scale production of Golden Dollar coins featuring Sacagawea began in November 1999. The coins started to appear in circulation two months later in January 2000.

---

*Step*
## 1

### Summary: The New Golden Dollar

When the vending machine industry began to see the benefits of one-dollar coins, the government's supply of Susan B. Anthony coins decreased. This led to President Clinton signing the "United States Dollar Coin Act of 1997." The act required the Treasury Department to put a new one-dollar coin into circulation. The coin had to be designed with specific features of size, color, and anti-counterfeiting properties. The back of the coin had to picture an eagle. The other side had to show one or more women who are no longer living.

The Dollar Coin Advisory Committee took suggestions from the public about the new coin's design. It was decided that the new coin would feature Sacagawea, the Native American who helped Lewis and Clark, explorers of the Northwestern United States. Production of the Golden Dollar began in November 1999, and the new coins were put into circulation in January 2000.

*Step*
## 2

There are several things to keep in mind as you plan to write a summary. Remember, a good summary:

- includes the main ideas
- eliminates unimportant or unnecessary information
- does not include many details
- is written in your own words

*Step*

*3*

Use the following prompt to complete the prewriting and writing activities:

**Read the passage "April Fool's Day" and write a summary.**

## April Fool's Day

Have you ever wondered where the tradition of playing silly pranks on April 1 began? Believe it or not, this holiday has been around for a long time. In France, during the early sixteenth century, the start of the new year was observed in early spring on April 1. To observe the holiday, the French danced and celebrated with festivities lasting late into the night, similar to the way people today celebrate New Year's Eve on December 31.

In the late 1500's, the Gregorian Calendar was introduced by King Charles IX of France. The new calendar moved New Year's Day to January 1. In those days, however, communication was poor. Most information was relayed by people traveling on foot. Thus, some of the French did not receive word of the calendar change until years after New Year's Day had been moved. These people, along with some of Charles's subjects who refused to celebrate January 1, continued to observe New Year's Day on April 1 and became known as "April fools." The fools were subject to pranks, ridicule, and practical jokes. The fools were given the name "Poisson d'Avril," meaning April fish, because at that time of the year, the sun was in the zodiac sign of Pisces, the fish.

The tradition of harassing and teasing people on April 1 continued long after January 1 became widely accepted as New Year's Day by the general population of France. French children would often put paper fish on their friends' backs and yell "Poisson d'Avril." The practice of playing small pranks on April 1 eventually spread to other European countries, including England and Scotland. By the eighteenth century, April Fool's Day had made its way to the American colonies of both England and France. April 1 became an international day for fun and jest.

April Fool's Day is a holiday that is still celebrated today. The small tricks people play are intended to be funny but never hurtful. Whenever a prankster successfully pulls off a trick, he or she yells, "April Fools!" The next time you fall for, or play, an April Fool's joke, think of the Poisson d'Avril who mistakenly observed April 1 as the first day of the new year in sixteenth century France.

**Step 4**

Complete the graphic organizer for a summary as your prewriting activity. Use your graphic organizer to help you think through your summary of "April Fool's Day."

*A full size graphic organizer can be found on page 102 of the Student Workbook.*

**STEPS FOR WRITING A SUMMARY**

Only The Main Ideas

Topic: _____

**Complete the Following Steps:**

Step 1 ❏ Skim the reading selection and begin to look for the main idea.

Step 2 ❏ Underline the topic sentence for each paragraph in the text selection. (If there is no topic sentence, write one for the paragraph.)

Step 3 ❏ Cross out unimportant information in the text selection.

Step 4 ❏ Cross out information that is repeated.

Step 5 ❏ Write what the text selection is about. Include only important information.

**Step 5**

Use the information from your graphic organizer to complete your summary. *(Students will have two pages to complete their writing activities.)*

**Writing Activity 15**

_____

_____

_____

_____

*Step*
*6*

The checklist shows what your best paper must have. Use the checklist below to review your work.

## Checklist for Writing Activity 15

❏ My summary has a sentence that identifies what the text selection is about.

❏ My summary is written in my own words.

❏ My summary states the main ideas of the text selection.

❏ My summary does not include information that is not important to the story.

❏ My summary is well organized and complete.

❏ I try to spell words correctly.

❏ I use words that make my meaning clear. I do not use the same words over and over.

❏ I use correct punctuation and capitalization.

❏ I have written my summary so the reader can read my print or cursive writing.

# Writing Activity 16: Summary

**Step 1**

Follow along as two passages are read aloud. The first passage is titled "My Big Game." The second passage is a summary of "My Big Game."

## My Big Game

It was the last game of the season, and my team, the Bobcats, was undefeated. We were playing the Hornets, the best team in the league. They were also undefeated. The game was tied 3-3 at the bottom of the ninth inning.

I knew I was the next person up to bat. I was beginning to feel knots twist the inside of my stomach. It's an honor for coach to trust me enough to bat at a time like this, I thought. I didn't want to let him or my team down.

I watched my teammate, Jeff, who was up at the plate. The sun hit his face, and I thought he looked confident. When the umpire yelled, "Strike!" for the third time, my stomach dropped. The pressure was all on me. It was the bottom of the ninth inning, and we had two outs. I took a deep breath and tried to look calm as I stepped up to the plate. The first pitch went wide; the second was a strike.

I felt myself become more nervous and took another deep breath to refocus. When the next pitch was thrown, I swung as hard as I could. I felt the ball make contact with my bat. "SNAP!" I threw my bat and headed for first base.

I was running as fast as my legs could carry me when I saw my coach jumping up and down and cheering from the sidelines. I looked toward the outfield and saw the ball fall over the fence. I had hit a home run! I ran around the diamond, touching first, second, and third base. As I approached home plate, I was greeted by my coach and my entire team! They lifted me onto their shoulders as everyone cheered. The day of the big game was the best day of my life!

*Step*
**1**

## Summary: My Big Game

Two undefeated baseball teams, the Bobcats and the Hornets, were playing their last game of the season. The game was tied 3-3 at the bottom of the ninth inning. After a teammate struck out, the author of the story was up to bat with two outs. On the third pitch, despite his nervousness, the author hit the ball as hard as he could. As he ran the bases, he looked up and saw the ball drop over the fence. He had scored a home run to win the game! The coach and team cheered for the batter as he approached home plate. They lifted the author onto their shoulders in celebration. The day of the big game was the best day of the author's life.

*Step*
**2**

There are several things to keep in mind as you plan to write a summary. Remember, a good summary:

- includes the main ideas
- eliminates unimportant or unnecessary information
- does not include many details
- is written in your own words

*Step*

# 3

Use the following prompt to complete the prewriting and writing activities:

**Read the passage "Malik's Machine" and write a summary.**

## Malik's Machine

When Malik's family saw his "time machine," they all laughed. Anybody would have laughed looking at the mass of cardboard and duct tape sitting in the Johnsons' backyard. There was nothing scientific about an old refrigerator box. "You're wasting your time," said Malik's brother, Jamal.

Alone in the yard, Malik looked at his time machine. There was a tear where his brother had lifted the hatch and tried to get inside. The cardboard was looking a little soggy from the morning dew. Even Malik had to admit it didn't look like much, but his mom always said to him, "What's on the outside does not matter; it's what's on the inside that counts."

Slowly, Malik climbed inside the main compartment and closed the hatch door carefully. After pressing a few buttons and setting a few dials, he pulled the final lever. As if it had come to life, the time machine churned and shook. Malik was glad he thought to install the seat belt. The time machine jumped and spun and finally, in a flash of light, Malik and his machine were gone.

When dinner time rolled around, Mrs. Johnson told Jamal to call Malik. Jamal peered into the backyard expecting to find Malik playing in his time machine, but Malik and the machine were both gone. Good, thought Jamal, that kid finally realized that playing 'time machine' was stupid and cleaned up his mess.

Jamal walked around the yard looking for Malik, when suddenly he was engulfed in a green fog. The ground beneath his feet began to shake. Jamal was scared, but soon everything stopped. Right in front of him was Malik's time machine. Jamal thought he was seeing things. That time machine had not been there two minutes ago. The hatch door popped open and out jumped his younger brother, all smiles. Malik handed him a piece of rope. When Jamal saw what was tied to the other end of the rope, his jaw dropped. He vowed he would never doubt his little brother again. There was a baby Triceratops sitting in the middle of his backyard.

*Step*

*4*

Complete the graphic organizer for a summary as your prewriting activity. Use your graphic organizer to help you think through your summary of "Malik's Machine."

*A full size graphic organizer can be found on page 110 of the Student Workbook.*

---

**STEPS FOR WRITING A SUMMARY**

Only The Main Ideas

Topic: _____

**Complete the Following Steps:**

Step 1 ☐ Skim the reading selection and begin to look for the main idea.

Step 2 ☐ Underline the topic sentence for each paragraph in the text selection. (If there is no topic sentence, write one for the paragraph.)

Step 3 ☐ Cross out unimportant information in the text selection.

Step 4 ☐ Cross out information that is repeated.

Step 5 ☐ Write what the text selection is about. Include only important information.

---

*Step*

*5*

Use the information from your graphic organizer to complete your summary. *(Students will have two pages to complete their writing activities.)*

**Writing Activity 16**

_____

_____

_____

_____

*Step*

**6**

The checklist shows what your best paper must have. Use the checklist below to review your work.

## Checklist for Writing Activity 16

❑ My summary has a sentence that identifies what the text selection is about.

❑ My summary is written in my own words.

❑ My summary states the main ideas of the text selection.

❑ My summary does not include information that is not important to the story.

❑ My summary is well organized and complete.

❑ I try to spell words correctly.

❑ I use words that make my meaning clear. I do not use the same words over and over.

❑ I use correct punctuation and capitalization.

❑ I have written my summary so the reader can read my print or cursive writing.

# Writing Activity 17: Thank-You Note

***Step***
**1**

Follow along as the thank-you note below is read aloud.

February 12, 2000

Dear Grandma and Grandpa,

I am writing to thank you for the inline skates you bought me for my birthday. I have been asking for a pair every birthday and holiday that I can remember. Mom and Dad always told me that I would have to wait until I was twelve, so I never dreamed I'd get the skates this year for my eleventh birthday.

When I opened my present from Mom and Dad, I thought a helmet and kneepads were strange gifts. After I tore open your package and saw those shiny, black inline skates lying in the middle of all of the packing peanuts and wrapping paper, their gifts made sense. Dad was afraid they had ruined the surprise for me, but I was so excited to have my own pair of inline skates, a year ahead of schedule, nothing could have ruined the day for me.

I pulled on the skates as soon as I kicked off my slippers. I must have looked funny trying to skate around the living room in my pajamas. Mom was not happy with the lines the wheels left in her new white carpet. She said that I could practice in the basement until the snow melts, but she didn't want anymore skating in her living room. Spring will be here soon though, and I can hardly wait to try them outside.

Thank you again for the great gift!

Love,

Cyrus

*Skating in the living room (sort of!)*

*Step*
**2**

Now you will do some organizing and planning for your own thank-you note. Remember that a good thank-you note has the following parts:

- the date
- a greeting or salutation
- a body
- a closing
- a signature

*Step*
**3**

Use the following prompt to complete the prewriting and writing activities:

> **A business person has donated money to your classroom for the purchase of computers. Write a thank-you note to this person, the president of a local company, for the generous donation. Explain why you are thankful and how you will use the new technology in your classroom.**

*Step*
**4**

Complete the graphic organizer for a thank-you note as your prewriting activity. Use your graphic organizer to help you think through your thank-you note.

*A full size graphic organizer can be found on page 116 of the Student Workbook.*

**THANK-YOU NOTE**

Date:

Greeting or Salutation:

Body — What you are thankful for and why:

Closing:

Signature:

*Step*

**5**

Use the information from your graphic organizer to complete your thank-you note. *(Students will have two pages to complete their writing activities.)*

### Writing Activity 17

*Step*

**6**

The checklist shows what your best paper must have. Use the checklist below to review your work.

### Checklist for Writing Activity 17

❑ I use the form for a letter with the date, a greeting, a body, a closing, and a signature.

❑ My thank-you note tells my reader why I am writing and makes a personal comment.

❑ My thank-you note explains why I am thankful.

❑ My thank-you note includes a personal closing comment.

❑ My thank-you note is well organized and complete.

❑ I try to spell words correctly.

❑ I use words that make my meaning clear. I do not use the same words over and over.

❑ I use correct punctuation and capitalization.

❑ I have written my thank-you note so the reader can read my print or cursive writing.

# Writing Activity 18: Thank-You Note

*Step*
**1** Follow along as the thank-you note below is read aloud.

March 6, 2000

Dear Mr. and Mrs. Parker,

Thank you for making me feel so welcome in your home last weekend. The trip to the amusement park on Saturday was so much fun! It was my first time riding roller coasters. The Beyond Gravity ride was as thrilling as everyone said it would be. I can't believe I learned how to surf at the water park's North Shore Adventure! The wave machine was really a wonder to see.

I told my mom how good Mr. Parker's chocolate chip pancakes tasted on Sunday morning. Mom said I've talked about that breakfast so much, she's going to call Mr. Parker for the recipe. Thank you again for making me a part of your family. I had a great time!

Sincerely,

Lu

in front of the Beyond Gravity roller coaster!

*Step*
2

Now you will do some organizing and planning for your own thank-you note. Remember that a good thank-you note has the following parts:

- the date
- a greeting or salutation
- a body
- a closing
- a signature

*Step*
3

Use the following prompt to complete the prewriting and writing activities:

> **Thank a friend, teacher, or family member for the support, kindness, or gesture of friendship he or she has shown you. Explain what you are thankful for and why.**

*Step*
4

Complete the graphic organizer for a thank-you note as your prewriting activity. Use your graphic organizer to help you think through your thank-you note.

*A full size graphic organizer can be found on page 122 of the Student Workbook.*

**THANK-YOU NOTE**

Date:

Greeting or Salutation:

Body — What you are thankful for and why:

Closing:

Signature:

*Step*
**5**
Use the information from your graphic organizer to complete your thank-you note. *(Students will have two pages to complete their writing activities.)*

### Writing Activity 18

_____

_____

_____

_____

*Step*
**6**
The checklist shows what your best paper must have. Use the checklist below to review your work.

### Checklist for Writing Activity 18

❏ I use the form for a letter with the date, a greeting, a body, a closing, and a signature.

❏ My thank-you note tells my reader why I am writing and makes a personal comment.

❏ My thank-you note explains why I am thankful.

❏ My thank-you note includes a personal closing comment.

❏ My thank-you note is well organized and complete.

❏ I try to spell words correctly.

❏ I use words that make my meaning clear. I do not use the same words over and over.

❏ I use correct punctuation and capitalization.

❏ I have written my thank-you note so the reader can read my print or cursive writing.

## Additional Writing Prompts for the Informational Report

Write a report on:

- a historic individual from North America or another region of the world.
- a simple mechanical device.
- a historical event in science that has impacted society.
- a form of government such as democracy, a monarchy, or dictatorship.
- changes that occur in the following: landforms, climate, natural vegetation, or natural resources.

## Additional Writing Prompts for the Summary

Write a summary for:

- a poem.
- an infomercial.
- a book read by the class.
- a magazine article.
- a play.
- a movie or television program.
- the purpose of an Internet web site.
- an encyclopedia entry.
- a documentary or docu-drama.
- an e-mail communication.
- a newscast.
- a newspaper article about a world, national, state, or local event.

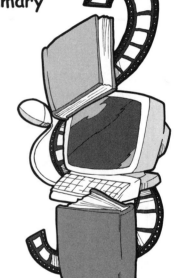

Note: Look for a variety of sources where students need to focus on the author's main purpose.

## Additional Writing Prompts for the Thank-You Note

Write a thank-you note:

- to someone for a gift.
- to someone who came to a special event for you.
- to someone who chaperoned a school dance, festival, or other school event.
- to someone who purchased something from you (such as a fund-raising item).
- to someone who donated time, materials, or money to your school.

# Chapter 5

# The Persuasive Communication Process
## (Letter to the Editor and Persuasive Paper)

## The Key Parts of this Chapter Include:

**1** Discussing the purpose and features of a letter to the editor and a persuasive paper.

**2** Showing how the persuasive communication process links to the eleven writing modes.

**3** Offering teaching tips on where students breakdown in the persuasive process.

**4** Providing ideas for the development of additional writing prompts for persuasive letters.

> The following teaching tools are provided for **letters to the editor** and **persuasive papers**: graphic organizers, models, two writing prompts, and student checklists.

## What is the Persuasive Communication Process?

The purpose of persuasion is to influence another person's or group's thinking about a particular issue. You can find examples of persuasive papers in editorial columns of newspapers or magazines, publications and position papers of special interest groups, infomercials, and other forms of advertising. Topics of persuasion often include current political and social issues.

### Features of a Letter to the Editor and a Persuasive Paper

- The writer must state his or her position on an issue.
- The writer must provide supporting evidence or reasons for the position taken.
- The reasons for writing a letter to the editor or persuasive paper should be logical and based on facts (not opinion).
- The writer must anticipate and acknowledge the "other side's point of view."
- A letter to the editor is written in the format of a letter.

**Persuasive Communication information for students can be found on page 127 of the *Write on Target* Student Workbook.**

## Language of Persuasion

| | | |
|---|---|---|
| It is my belief that… | On the other hand | What is your point? |
| In my opinion… | State | However |
| As noted… | Opinion | Yet |
| As you can see… | I see your point | I doubt |
| In conclusion… | For these reasons | Argue |
| Pro | Point of view | Con |

## Correlation of Persuasive Communication to the Writing Modes

**Letter to the Editor** – a piece of writing in the form of a letter, including greeting, body and closing, that expresses the writer's opinion and why it is important. The writer's opinion should be based on facts, examples and/or reasons. The writer should also include what he/she would like to see happen.

**Persuasive** – a piece of writing that states a position on an issue and attempts to convince the audience to agree with the writer. This is accomplished by providing supporting evidence or reasons for the position taken based on facts. An important part of a persuasive piece is anticipating the other side's point of view.

## Teaching Tips:
## Where Students Breakdown in the Persuasive Communication Process

• Students do not understand the difference between fact and opinion.

• Students fail to recognize that there can be a variety of possible positions; there is rarely one "right" position.

• The reasons that students give to influence somebody else's thinking must be based on facts and not just personal opinion.

• Some students are unable to see the position from the other side's point of view.

• Students do not have enough information to argue a position.

pros        cons

# Writing Activity 19: Letter to the Editor

*Step*

# 1

Follow along as the letter to the editor below is read aloud.

May 30, 2000

Dear Editor,

I am writing to bring to your attention the need for a city-wide effort to "clean up" our community. Litter is filling our streets, our parks, and our neighborhoods. Does anyone in City Hall have a plan for tackling this litter problem?

We need to set a positive image for members of our community. We need to let people know we are proud of where we live, and littering in our community is wrong. I want my little brothers and sisters to grow up in a clean and safe community.

I am making three recommendations for City Hall to consider regarding this littering problem:

1. Place more trash cans around the city to discourage people from disposing of their trash on the ground.
2. Pass a city law that fines anyone who litters.
3. Display "Don't Litter" and "Keep Our Neighborhood Clean" awareness signs throughout the city.

I hope that City Hall and the residents of our community will think long and hard about a solution to this growing litter problem.

Sincerely,

Everett Meyers

*Step* **2**

Now you will do some organizing and planning for your own letter to the editor. Remember that a good letter to the editor has the following parts:

- a greeting, a body, a closing, and a signature
- a statement of your opinion
- support for your opinion with facts and statements
- a conclusion that restates your opinion (it may include a suggestion for what needs to be done)

*Step* **3**

Use the following prompt to complete the prewriting and writing activities:

> **Write a letter to the editor of your community newspaper. Take a stand for or against the following issue: there should be more activities for young people in our community.**

*Step* **4**

Complete the graphic organizer for a letter to the editor as your prewriting activity. Use your graphic organizer to help you think through your letter to the editor.

*A full size graphic organizer can be found on page 130 of the Student Workbook.*

**LETTER TO THE EDITOR**

Date:

Greeting:

Personal comment (include why you are writing)

Details

First:

Second:

Third:

Personal comments ending the letter (include a restatement of why you are writing)

Closing:

Signature:

*Step*

**5**

Use the information from your graphic organizer to complete your letter to the editor. *(Students will have two pages to complete their writing activities.)*

### Writing Activity 19

_____

_____

_____

_____

_____

*Step*

**6**

The checklist shows what your best paper must have. Use the checklist below to review your work.

### Checklist for Writing Activity 19

❏ My letter tells why I am writing this letter to the editor.

❏ My letter tells why I believe my opinion or information is important.

❏ I state my opinion with facts and examples or important reasons.

❏ I restate my opinion in my conclusion and say what I would like to happen.

❏ I use the form for a letter with a date, a greeting, a body, a closing, and a signature.

❏ My letter to the editor is well organized and complete.

❏ I use words that make my meaning clear. I do not use the same words over and over again.

❏ I try to spell words correctly.

❏ I use correct punctuation and capitalization.

❏ I have written with my best handwriting in print or in cursive.

# Writing Activity 20: Letter to the Editor

*Step*
## 1

Follow along as the letter to the editor below is read aloud.

September 5, 2000

Dear Editor,

I am writing this letter to bring your attention to the need for more sidewalks in our city's neighborhoods. Due to the lack of sidewalks, our residents risk danger each time they walk, jog, or inline skate on our city streets.

In addition, traffic is becoming more and more congested as car and truck drivers come to near halts when attempting to pass a runner or cyclist. I am concerned for the safety of people in this community, especially when pedestrians and motorists are forced to use the same roadways.

Neighborhoods throughout our community consist of families, many with young children. It is important for these children to have safe areas to skate and walk. Many children, who are not permitted on streets, walk through neighbors' lawns.

I know there are several people in my neighborhood whose grass is being trampled because of repeated foot traffic from neighborhood kids. I'm sure these community members would really appreciate more sidewalks on which children could travel.

We must make a change for the safety and convenience of our community members. My grandfather tells me a Development Trust was set up a few years ago to enrich this community. Please consider using money from the trust to build more sidewalks. Thank you for considering my recommendation.

Sincerely,

Nadia Rees

*Step*

*2*

Now you will do some organizing and planning for your own letter to the editor. Remember that a good letter to the editor has the following parts:

- a greeting, body, a closing, and a signature
- a statement of your opinion
- support for your opinion with facts and statements
- a conclusion that restates your opinion (it may include a suggestion for what needs to be done)

*Step*

*3*

Use the following prompt to complete the prewriting and writing activities:

**Many students feel it is important to wear the latest designer clothing that is often very expensive. Write a letter to the editor of your school newspaper. In your letter, take a position on this statement: "Who you are is more important than what you wear."**

*Step*

*4*

Complete the graphic organizer for a letter to the editor as your prewriting activity. Use your graphic organizer to help you think through your letter to the editor.

*A full size graphic organizer can be found on page 136 of the Student Workbook.*

**LETTER TO THE EDITOR**

Date:

Greeting:

Personal comment (include why you are writing)

**Details**

First:

Second:

Third:

Personal comments ending the letter (include a restatement of why you are writing)

Closing:

Signature:

**Step 5** Use the information from your graphic organizer to complete your letter to the editor. *(Students will have two pages to complete their writing activities.)*

### Writing Activity 20

_____

_____

_____

_____

**Step 6** The checklist shows what your best paper must have. Use the checklist below to review your work.

### Checklist for Writing Activity 20

☐ My letter tells why I am writing this letter to the editor.

☐ My letter tells why I believe my opinion or information is important.

☐ I state my opinion with facts and examples or important reasons.

☐ I restate my opinion in my conclusion and say what I would like to happen.

☐ I use the form for a letter with a date, a greeting, a body, a closing, and a signature.

☐ My letter to the editor is well organized and complete.

☐ I use words that make my meaning clear. I do not use the same words over and over again.

☐ I try to spell words correctly.

☐ I use correct punctuation and capitalization.

☐ I have written with my best handwriting in print or in cursive.

# Writing Activity 21: Persuasive Paper

*Step*
**1**
Follow along as the persuasive piece below is read aloud.

### Skateboarders' Dilemma

I believe that skateboarders in our community are not being treated fairly. Skateboarding is a wholesome outdoor sport and a great form of exercise. More and more of my peers are becoming worried about the fact that skateboarding is being banned all over our town.

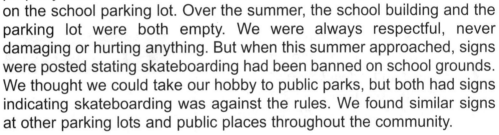

My friends and I have searched everywhere for a place to skateboard and are constantly being told we are not permitted to skate on private or public property. Last summer we skateboarded on the school parking lot. Over the summer, the school building and the parking lot were both empty. We were always respectful, never damaging or hurting anything. But when this summer approached, signs were posted stating skateboarding had been banned on school grounds. We thought we could take our hobby to public parks, but both had signs indicating skateboarding was against the rules. We found similar signs at other parking lots and public places throughout the community.

Skateboarding is a sport just like any other that requires a great deal of skill and practice. We feel skateboarders are being treated unfairly. Bicycling, jogging, and inline skating are allowed in public parks, but skateboarding is not. If you are going to ban skateboarding from public places, please give kids somewhere they can skateboard.

The neighboring community of Sierra built a skateboarding complex for local teens about two years ago. The money to build the complex was raised by teens and their families as well as members of the Parks and Recreation Board, the mayor, and his staff. The skateboarding area in Sierra is a huge success. The skateboarders respect the area and often invite members of the community to watch their practice sessions. The area helps everyone appreciate this unique sport.

I think our community should consider building a skateboarding area. The area would provide a safe place for kids to skateboard and have fun with their peers. If we look at the example set by the community of Sierra, we can see that a skateboarding area is a good idea for our town.

*Step*
**2**

Now you will do some organizing and planning for your own persuasive paper. Remember that a good persuasive paper has the following parts:

- a statement of your opinion
- support for your opinion with facts and statements
- a conclusion that restates your opinion (it may include a suggestion for what needs to be done)

*Step*
**3**

Use the following prompt to complete the prewriting and writing activities:

**Choose an important issue facing your community, state, or country. Write a persuasive paper that will convince the reader to agree with your opinion.**

*Step*
**4**

Complete the graphic organizer for a persuasive paper as your prewriting activity. Use your graphic organizer to help you think through your persuasive paper.

*A full size graphic organizer can be found on page 142 of the Student Workbook.*

**PERSUASIVE PAPER**

Title: _____

Introductory Paragraph (State your opinion.)

Reason #1:

Reason #2:

Reason #3:

Concluding Paragraph

**Step 5**

Use the information from your graphic organizer to complete your persuasive paper. *(Students will have two pages to complete their writing activities.)*

## Writing Activity 21

_____

_____

_____

_____

_____

**Step 6**

The checklist shows what your best paper must have. Use the checklist below to review your work.

## Checklist for Writing Activity 21

❑ My persuasive paper has a statement of my opinion.

❑ I support my opinion with facts, examples, and important reasons.

❑ I organize my support in paragraphs.

❑ I use signal words (first, next, then, in addition, consequently, etc.) that make my writing easy to follow.

❑ I have a conclusion that restates my opinion and says what needs to be done.

❑ My persuasive paper is well organized and complete.

❑ I use words that make my meaning clear. I do not use the same words over and over again.

❑ I try to spell words correctly.

❑ I use correct punctuation and capitalization.

❑ I have written with my best handwriting in print or in cursive.

# Writing Activity 22: Persuasive Paper

*Step*

# 1

Follow along as the persuasive piece below is read aloud.

### Keesha Smith for Student Council Representative

My name is Keesha Smith, and I am running for Student Council. I think that I would be a good Student Council representative for the students of our school.

I have new and interesting ideas on how we could make improvements in our school. First, I would like to petition the school board to use some of the money from the spring fundraiser to buy new computers for the library. I believe students need to be able to work with computers as much as possible before they go to high school. Second, I would like to start a school newspaper club. All students would be invited to join the club. The newspaper would be a good way to promote the positive things going on in our school. It would also help to keep everyone informed.

Another reason I feel that I would be a good representative on Student Council is I get along well with most people in school, including teachers and other school employees. This would make it easy for me to talk with people about the changes and ideas that I have. I am outgoing and caring, and I will make sure I listen to everyone's ideas. I think that an important part of being on Student Council is listening to the ideas and concerns of students in our school. I promise to bring all those ideas and suggestions to the Student Council's attention. I will work together with other members of the Student Council to make our school the best that it can be.

I have been going to this school since I was in first grade, so I know pretty well how things work around here. I know that Student Council is an important part of our school, and I believe I would be a good representative for the student body. Please keep the name Keesha Smith in mind when you vote for Student Council representatives next week.

*Step* **2**
Now you will do some organizing and planning for your own persuasive paper. Remember that a good persuasive paper has the following parts:

- a statement of your opinion
- support for your opinion with facts and statements
- a conclusion that restates your opinion (it may include a suggestion for what needs to be done)

*Step* **3**
Use the following prompt to complete the prewriting and writing activities:

> **Choose an important issue facing your school or family. Write a persuasive paper that will convince the reader to agree with your opinion.**

*Step* **4**
Complete the graphic organizer for a persuasive paper as your prewriting activity. Use your graphic organizer to help you think through your persuasive paper.

*A full size graphic organizer can be found on page 148 of the Student Workbook.*

**PERSUASIVE PAPER**

Title: _____

**Introductory Paragraph (State your opinion.)**

**Reason #1:**

**Reason #2:**

**Reason #3:**

**Concluding Paragraph**

**Step 5**

Use the information from your graphic organizer to complete your persuasive paper. *(Students will have two pages to complete their writing activities.)*

### Writing Activity 22

_____

_____

_____

_____

**Step 6**

The checklist shows what your best paper must have. Use the checklist below to review your work.

### Checklist for Writing Activity 22

❑ My persuasive paper has a statement of my opinion.

❑ I support my opinion with facts, examples, and important reasons.

❑ I organize my support in paragraphs.

❑ I use signal words (first, next, then, in addition, consequently, etc.) that make my writing easy to follow.

❑ I have a conclusion that restates my opinion and says what needs to be done.

❑ My persuasive paper is well organized and complete.

❑ I use words that make my meaning clear. I do not use the same words over and over again.

❑ I try to spell words correctly.

❑ I use correct punctuation and capitalization.

❑ I have written with my best handwriting in print or in cursive.

## Additional Writing Prompts for Letters to the Editor

**1.** Academic achievement rarely receives the recognition it deserves.

**2.** Speed limits should be lowered or raised.

**3.** Schools should be equally funded throughout the state.

**4.** All people should have the opportunity to vote.

**5.** All pet owners should be required to obtain a license for their pets, including cats, dogs, birds, and hamsters.

**6.** There should be a law requiring advertising to be truthful.

## Additional Writing Prompts for Persuasive Papers

Take a stand on one of these national, state, local, or school issues and persuade your reader to agree with you regarding:

- cafeteria food.
- school dress codes.
- the value of athletic programs.
- the importance of art and music.
- the length of the school year.
- seat belt laws.
- increased or decreased bicycle safety laws.
- buying products made in America.
- a law stating children under the age of 16 must be accompanied by an adult at the mall.
- ratings on music lyrics, video games, computer software, or television shows.

## Additional Writing Prompts for Persuasive Papers, Continued

Take a stand on one of these family issues and persuade your family to agree with you.

- When your family spends an evening together, you always play the same games. Persuade members of your family to try a new game.

- Your family has decided to get a pet. Decide what kind of pet you would like to have. Persuade your family that your idea for the family's new pet is a good choice.

- Your best friend who moved to another state has invited you to come and stay with his or her family for one week. You need to fly alone on an airplane to get there. Persuade your parents to let you fly by yourself so you can visit your friend.

- A holiday is fast approaching. For the past several years, your family has eaten the same meal, but this year you would like to have something different. Persuade your family that a new menu for the holiday dinner is a good idea.

- You have the same bedtime as a sibling who is two years younger than you. Persuade your parents to extend your bedtime.

- You think you deserve a larger allowance. Convince someone that you deserve more money.

- You feel you have too many or too few chores around the house. Persuade a family member to agree with you.

- You would like to go to see a movie with a group of friends. Why should your parents let you go out with your friends?

# Chapter 6

# Additional Resources

The following titles will provide support for additional sources of models for each of the communication processes. You may want to utilize sections with your students to examine the features of the communication process as a reading or "read aloud" selection, or you may use an individual title in its entirety for classroom study. The model lesson from *Write on Target* can be paired with the appropriate graphic organizer and a model from the text for an easy-to-plan writing lesson. This list of titles is not meant to be comprehensive; you will add to the list with materials from your own classroom.

**Titles to support the *Narrative Communication Process***

| | |
|---|---|
| Armstrong, William H. | Sounder |
| Atwater, Richard | Mr. Popper's Penguins |
| Babbitt, Natalie | Tuck Everlasting |
| Bauer, Joan | Sticks |
| Fletcher, Ralph | Fig Pudding |
| London, Jack | White Fang |
| Lewis, C.S. | The Lion, the Witch, & the Wardrobe |
| O'Dell, Scott | Island of the Blue Dolphins |
| Paulsen, Gary | Mr. Tucket |
| | Brian's Winter |
| Sachar, Louis | Holes |
| Tillage, Leon Walter | Leon's Story |

## Titles to Support the *Descriptive Communication Process*

| | |
|---|---|
| George, Jean Craighead | Julie of the Wolves |
| L'Engle, Madeleine | A Wrinkle in Time |
| Kerr, M.E. | Gentlehands |
| Lasky, Kathryn | The Most Beautiful Roof in the World |
| Levine, Gail Carson | Ella Enchanted |
| London, Jack | The Call of the Wild |
| Napoli, Donna Jo | The Prince of the Pond |
| Pinkney, Andrea Davis | Duke Ellington: The Piano Prince and His Orchestra |
| Rawls, Wilson | Where the Red Fern Grows |
| Spinelli, Jerry | Wringer |
| Steinbeck, John | The Gift |
| | The Red Pony |
| Wrede, Patricia C. | Dealing with Dragons |

## Titles to Support the *Direction Communication Process*

| | |
|---|---|
| Maestro, B. and G. | Exploration and Conquest: The Americas After Columbus |
| Raskin, Ellen | The Westing Game |
| Rockwell, Thomas | How to Eat Fried Worms |
| Schaefer, Jack | Old Ramon |
| Stevenson, Robert Louis | Treasure Island |
| Stockton, Frank | The Lady or the Tiger |
| Tsuchiya, Yukio | Faithful Elephants |
| Zaunders, Bo | Crocodiles, Camels, and Dugout Canoes |

## Titles to Support the *Explanation Communication Process*

| | |
|---|---|
| Byars, Betsy Cromer | The Summer of the Swans |
| George, Jean Craighead | The Moon of the Salamanders |
| Jones, Charlotte Foltz | Accidents May Happen: Fifty Inventions Discovered by Mistake |
| Kipling, Rudyard | Just So Stories |
| Lord, Walter | A Night to Remember |
| Macaulay, David | The New Way Things Work |
| Micucci, Charles | The Life and Times of the Peanut |
| Rylant, Cynthia | A Fine White Dust |
| Tanaka, Shelley | Discovering the Iceman |
| Wilder, Laura Ingalls | The Little House on the Prairie Series |

## Titles to Support the *Persuasive Communication Process*

| | |
|---|---|
| Avi | The Barn |
| | What Do Fish Have to Do with Anything? |
| De Maupassant, Guy | The Necklace |
| Hesse, Karen | The Music of Dolphins |
| Ingle, Annie | Robin Hood |
| Orwell, George | Animal Farm |
| Robinson, Barbara | The Best Christmas Pageant Ever |
| Scieszka, John | The True Story of the Three Little Pigs |
| Twain, Mark | The Celebrated Jumping Frog of Calaveras County |

# A New Book Series

# Write on Target

## Using Graphic Organizers to Improve Writing Skills

Series written by:
Yolande Grizinski, Ed.D.
Leslie Holzhauser-Peters, MS, CCC-SP

| item# | description | isbn | price |
|-------|-------------|------|-------|
| NA1341 | Gr. 3-4 Parent/Teacher Edition | 1-884183-55-7 | $16.95 |
| NA1342 | Gr. 3-4 Student Workbook | 1-884183-56-5 | $10.95 |
| NA1343 | Classroom Set** | | $275.00 |

| item# | description | isbn | price |
|-------|-------------|------|-------|
| NA1561 | Gr. 5-6 Parent/Teacher Edition | 1-884183-57-3 | $16.95 |
| NA1562 | Gr. 5-6 Student Workbook | 1-884183-58-1 | $10.95 |
| NA1563 | Classroom Set** | | $275.00 |

## Parent/Teacher Edition

Teach students to write effectively and improve writing skills with this two book series for Grades 3 and 4 and Grades 5 and 6. *Write on Target* offers a step-by-step guide with a lesson plan framework and tools for teaching the writing process to multi-grade levels. Writing activities cover five communication processes and the eleven modes of writing. These books can also be used in year-long writing programs, in assessment, for intervention, and for individual practice.

## Student Workbook

To improve students' writing skills, these workbooks contain over 20 model lessons and prompts to cover fictional and personal narratives, journal writing, letter writing, directions, invitations, thank-you notes, summaries, informational reports, letters to the editor, and more. Students will use a six-step process, to successfully address each prompt, which includes reading, pre-writing, writing, and checklists.

**A Classroom Set includes 1 Parent/Teacher Edition and 30 Student Workbooks.

# Call 1-877-PASSING or Visit www.eapublishing.com